ISIS vs. the Illuminati

The War for a New World Order

The Dark Lords

Black Temple Publishing

Black Temple Publishing
thedarklords.com

CONTENTS

INTRODUCTION

A New World War

There is a war underway for the souls of mankind and the future of the world. Two opposing visions of civilization, religion, morality and culture are clashing on battlefields across the globe – perhaps on the streets of a city near you. It is a war that is being waged at every level: military, religious, ideological, cultural, economic and demographic. Security forces, militant cells, religious leaders, scholars, analysts, artists, "lone-wolves" and ordinary citizens are being called upon to take sides and to take up arms to protect their way of life. An age of apocalyptic world war, it seems, is dawning across the world.

This war is different than recent major conflicts; its origins goes back centuries, into the most deeply rooted myths and power structures of two great civilizations. It is not being fought over superficial differences of territory, tribe, political ideology or nationality, but over fundamental differences of worldview, religion and philosophy. As we shall show, it is in fact a war between two great world domination projects: the *Islamic State* and the *Illuminati*. This book is an attempt to make sense of this great global conflict, and to explain the players, stakes and ideas behind a deadly game that will no doubt define our world for many years to come.

A Third Perspective

Many books have been written about the conflict between Islamism, jihadism, al Qaeda, ISIS, etc. and the "West" or the "modern world". They often have sensationalist styles and read like propaganda for the "War on Terror" or apologetics for the global jihad. But few books have examined both sides of the conflict from a more neutral point of view, and sought to get at the deeper roots of the conflict. What exactly are the ideas, agendas and power structures of the Westernized world that the Islamists object to, and vice versa? Who are the main players driving the war? What are their histories, myths and metaphysical beliefs? What strategies and tactics are they using to achieve victory?

This is not a "blame the West first" book of equivocations and apologetics; nor is it an "Islamophobic" screed about the evils of Islamic civilization; nor is it a book of Islamist propaganda. Rather, it is a calm inquiry into the deep power structures and ideologies that animate the militants on both sides, which I hope will give the reader a perspective they haven't encountered before. One thing I do know is this: in every conflict there are propagandists posing as objective analysts, and two sides to every story. I do not claim to be objective, but I do intend to cut through some of the propaganda and provide some insight into why both sides fight in the great conflict of our time: the war between the Islamists and the Illuminati for a New World Order.

WHO IS ISIS?

The first player in this great global drama is *ISIS* – an acronym for **Islamic State of Iraq and al-Sham**. ISIS is a militant jihadist organization based in Iraq and Syria that declared the establishment of an Islamic Caliphate on June 29, 2014. They have gained global notoriety for their videotaped beheadings, terrorist attacks, suicide bombings, mass executions, sexual enslavement, crucifixions, stonings and other atrocities. They have declared their intention to wage holy war until the entire world has submitted to their extreme version of Islam.

History of ISIS

ISIS evolved from an organization founded by a Jordanian named Abu Musab al-Zarqawi in the late 1990s, which became *al Qaeda in Iraq* and pledged allegiance to Osama bin Laden in 2004. The group declared the founding of the *Islamic State in Iraq (ISI)* in 2006 and quickly became a dominant force among Sunni militant groups there. However, the group was soon decimated by American Special Operations, the American troop surge and the "Anbar Awakening" tribal uprising. By 2011, ISI was reduced to isolated cells with no centralized command structure, and was effectively defeated.

However, with the pull-out of US troops and the able leadership of Abu Bakr al-Baghdadi, ISI rapidly rebuilt its capabilities. The outbreak of civil war in Syria in 2011 and a prison break campaign in 2012 helped the group greatly expand its manpower and operations. In 2013, it renamed itself *Islamic State of Iraq and the Levant (ISIL/ISIS)* and gained considerable support among Sunni tribes. ISIS formally split with al Qaeda in 2014 after al-Baghdadi refused to obey al Qaeda leader Ayman al-Zawahiri's order to disband. With the declaration of their Caliphate in 2014, ISIS simplified its name to *Islamic State (IS)* to reflect its global ambitions. Since then, the group has attracted thousands of recruits, established dozens of *wilayah* (provinces), and perpetrated or inspired numerous high profile terrorist attacks around the world.

How was ISIS able to rise so quickly from the ashes of defeat to become a global menace? Four major factors have been identified: incompetence of Iraqi security forces, innovative tactics, the resentment of marginalized Sunnis, and ideological appeal. The last factor is the one we're most interested in, and is the one that has propelled ISIS ahead of al Qaeda as the most powerful jihadist group in the world. By taking territory and building a state, ISIS is showing that it can do more than hide in caves in Afghanistan and make threats. What al Qaeda has long wanted to do – establish an Islamic Caliphate – ISIS has now done. And their unprecedented ability to use social media such as twitter, youtube and facebook to spread their message has enabled them to infect the minds of young people throughout the globe. This has made their Islamic State a magnet for jihadists from all over the world who are looking for a radical alternative to the way of life promoted in the West.

ISIS IDEOLOGY

What ideas and currents of thought have led to the ISIS phenomenon? Let us look at some of the most important ideological sources to get a better understanding of what motivates and informs ISIS.

Islam

ISIS are followers of *Islam*, a religion that came into existence following the revelations of the self-declared prophet Muhammad that began in 610 C.E. Muhammad's revelations, which he claimed were communicated to him from *Allah*, the one almighty God, were recorded in a book called the *Quran*. The Quran claims to be the completion of the monotheistic religion that began with the revelations of Moses, continued with Jesus, and were perfected by Muhammad, the final messenger of God. Muslims also follow the *Sunnah* – the deeds, sayings and way of life of Muhammad, as recorded by his companions in the *hadiths* (accounts of the Prophet).

Islam offers mankind a stark choice: obey the commands of Allah, as transmitted to Muhammad and the previous prophets and recorded in the Quran and the hadiths, or risk burning in the Hellfire of *Jahannam* for eternity. If one stays on the "Straight Path" of Islam, one may be admitted to *Jenna*, an otherworldly paradise where one will live in bliss among beautiful virgins, fine foods, gardens and golden houses for all eternity. To stay on the Straight Path, the Muslim must obey the five pillars of Islam:

- Shahada: The declaration of faith taken by all Muslims: "There is no god but God (and) Muhammad is the messenger of God."
- Salat: The five daily prayers.
- Zakat: regular charitable donations to the Muslim community.
- Sawm: Fasting during Ramadan, and at other times.
- Hajj: making a pilgrimage to Mecca during the twelfth month of the Islamic calendar at least one in a lifetime.

The key Islamic principle is *Tawheed:* pure monotheism of one god, with no partners and no idolatry. The Muslim must only do that which is *halal* – permitted by Allah – and avoid doing that which is *haram* – forbidden by Allah – as revealed in the Quran and the Sunna. This is the religion of Islam in a nutshell.

Jihad

The Quran contains a number of verses that can be interpreted in a militant manner. For example, *Surah* (verse) 9:29 commands:

> Fight those who do not believe in Allah or in the Last Day and who do not consider unlawful what Allah and His Messenger have made unlawful and who do not adopt the religion of truth from those who were given the Scripture - [fight] until they give the jizyah [tax] willingly while they are humbled.

Surah 9:33 continues:

> He it is who sent His Messenger with guidance and

the religion of truth, that He may make it prevail over every other religion, even though the idolaters may dislike it.

In a 'strong' hadith (a reliable account of the Prophet), Muhammad makes the following prophecy:

"Verily Allah has shown me the eastern and western part of the earth, and I saw the authority of my Ummah (nation) dominate ALL that I saw."

Verses like these are interpreted by jihadists to mean that Muslims have been commanded by God to make the entire world submit to His religion, and they must therefore wage *jihad* (holy war) until they have conquered the world for Islam.   In fact, jihad as been called the "sixth pillar" of Islam and the "forgotten obligation" by some Islamist scholars. This is justified by verses such Surah 9:111:

Surely Allah has purchased of the believers their lives and their belongings and in return has promised that they shall have Paradise. They fight in the Way of Allah, and slay and are slain. Such is the promise He has made incumbent upon Himself in the Torah, and the Gospel, and the Qur'an. Who is more faithful to his promise than Allah? Rejoice, then, in the bargain you have made with Him. That indeed is the mighty triumph.

In a reliable hadith, Muhammad is recorded as saying:

Paradise has one hundred grades which Allah has reserved for the Mujahidun who fight in Allah's Cause, and the distance between each of two grades is like the distance between heaven and the earth. So when you ask Allah (for something), ask for the Al-Firdaus which is the middle (best) and the highest part of Paradise.

While many Muslims argue that "jihad" refers to an inner struggle against one's sinful nature, verses like the above make it clear that fighting is also prescribed for Muslims, and indeed may guarantee their entry into the most exalted realms of Paradise. This is why jihadists are often so fervent in their desire to wage jihad, and willing to sacrifice their lives for the sake of Allah.

Sharia

The goal of ISIS and other Islamist groups is the implementation of *Sharia* in all Muslim societies. Sharia is the Islamic legal system, derived from the Quran, the Sunnah and the reasoning of Islamic scholars from those sources. As such, it is a divine, perfect, eternal basis for society, which can never be altered or made subject to man-made law. Sharia governs all aspects of a Muslim's life, from politics to economics to waging war to acceptable social conduct to personal behavior such as prayer, diet, hygiene and sexuality. After a few centuries of development, Sharia became standardized, and was implemented across the Muslim world for around eight hundred years. However, the intrusion of Western colonial regimes into the Muslim world led to the introduction of Western ideas such as secularism, democracy and nationalism and the break-down of the Sharia system in modern times.

At the present time, no society in the world implements Sharia fully. Afghanistan came close under Taliban rule in the 1990s, but that was ended by the American invasion after 9/11. Even Saudi Arabia, often considered the strictest Islamic society, violates Sharia by allowing banks to collect interest on their territory – interest *(Riba)* being forbidden under Islamic law. ISIS claims they are implementing Sharia fully in their "Islamic State", but many scholars disagree, pointing to the violence they practice against non-Muslims, slavery, destruction and totalitarianism as being violations of Islamic laws and traditions.

Salafism

Salafism is the school of Islamic thought that has most influenced ISIS, al Qaeda, and many other militant groups. It is a puritanical interpretation of Islam that traces its lineage to a medieval Syrian scholar named Ibn Taymiyya. Salafis preach against all forms of innovation and idolatry introduced into the religion after Muhammad and his early companions and successors (called *the Salaf*). They strive to adhere rigorously to the letter of the Quran and Sunnah, and also to revive the manner of dress, speaking and other cultural practices of the Salaf. Not all Salafis are militant or politically-oriented; many are "quietists" who are focused on the theological and cultural dimensions of reviving pure Islam in the modern world. However, a subset of Salafis called *Salafi jihadists* are focused on the militant, physical warfare dimension of Islamic revival. This includes ISIS, al Qaeda and many other violent Islamist factions. As an aggressive, expansionist global movement with significant financial and theological support, Salafi jihadism is the leading source of Islamist militancy in the world today.

Wahhabism

One particular current of Salafist thought that has

strongly influenced the ideology of ISIS originated with an Arab scholar named Muhammad ibn ʿAbd al-Wahhab. In the mid-18th century, around the same time that Europeans like Voltaire and Weishaupt were developing the intellectual foundations of the Enlightenment and the Illuminati, Wahhab was creating its antithesis: the austere, radical form of Islam that has come to be known as *Wahhabism*.

Wahhabism is a radical doctrine that rejects the entire traditional system of Islamic law that was developed by Muslim scholars over several centuries following Muhammad's death. Wahhab taught that every generation of Muslims after the Salaf had deviated further from true Islam and fallen into decadence and *kufr* (unbelief). To Wahhab, the Muslim world was in need of a revolution – a purging of infidels, idolatry and innovation and a return to its primary sources (the Quran and Sunnah). One method Wahhab encouraged was to make *takfir* – to declare another Muslim an apostate for violating Wahhab's strict version of Islam – a crime punishable by death. Another method of revitalization would be *jihad* – holy war – both within Arabia and outward against the Ottoman Empire that ruled the Muslim world at that time.

Three Wahhabi Waves

Wahhab's ideology would be put into practice after 1744, when Muhammad bin Saud, founder of the Saudi dynasty, made an alliance with the preacher and began their campaign to conquer Arabia. Since that fateful alliance, there have been three major outbreaks of ISIS-style Wahhabi violence, including the current one ravaging Iraq and Syria.

The first Wahhabi outbreak came in 1801, when the Saudis raided Karbala in Iraq and massacred thousands of Shiite men, women and children. They then entered Mecca and Medina in 1803, which surrendered due to the terror the Wahhabis had instilled in the population. The onslaught on the peninsula continued for another decade, until it was crushed by the armies of the Ottoman Turks who controlled most of Arabia at the time.

A century later, a second Wahhabi outbreak challenged Ottoman Turk rule and menaced the region with the specter of expansionist jihad. Beginning during World War I, the *Ikhwan* Wahhabi militia, still allied with the Saudi family, succeeded in expelling the Ottoman Turks with the cooperation of the British. They went on to conquer Mecca, Medina and most of the Arabian peninsula in the 1920s, and like ISIS today, threatened to expand their jihad across the region. This second Wahhabi outbreak was crushed by the Saudis themselves, with the cooperation of the British. For most of another century, the Wahhabis laid dormant, until the events of the early 21st century awakened them for their third onslaught, in the form of *ISIS*.

The Final Battle

In the hadiths, it is prophesied that there will be a great final battle called *al-Mahama* with *Rum (Rome)* in the last days before the Day of Judgement. Here 'Rome' is interpreted to mean Europe, America or the West as a whole. It is predicted that the great battle will begin in *Dabiq*, a town in modern-day Syria. Dabiq happens to be one of the first towns that ISIS conquered during is initial expansion, despite its strategic unimportance. ISIS also named its English language magazine after the city, and features this quote from its founder in every issue: "The spark has been lit here in Iraq, and its heat will continue to intensify – by Allah's permission – until it burns the crusader armies in Dabiq." Now ISIS wants to provoke Rome to invade, which will light the fire of the final battle in Dabiq as prophesied. For it is further prophesied that the Muslims will defeat Rome at Dabiq, and drive them back to Istanbul. After that, the *Dajjal* (Islamic Anti-Christ) will appear in Jerusalem, and the final tribulations before Judgement Day will begin. This will mark the literal end of time, and the destruction of the whole universe created by Allah. From their words and deeds, ISIS clearly believes that they could be the Muslim army that defeats Rome and battles the Dajjal at the End of Days – which makes them more than a radical Islamist force; it makes them a *doomsday cult*.

THE ISLAMIST ELITE

The version of Islam which has culminated in ISIS is often called *Islamism* – an aggressive interpretation of the religion which is primarily concerned with acquiring political and military power. There are a number of key thinkers and organizations who have developed and propagated Islamism; we discuss some of the most important below.

Islamist Organizations
The Muslim Brotherhood

The Muslim Brotherhood, founded in 1928, is a highly influential Islamist political organization that has tens of thousands of members and branches throughout the Muslim world. The group's goals include the introduction of Sharia into Muslim societies, the toppling of non-Islamic governments in Muslim lands, and the re-establishment of the Caliphate. The Brotherhood has been engaged in a long struggle against the government of Egypt, which it views as a non-Islamic Western puppet, and has been instrumental in several coups, assassinations and revolutions in the Arab world.

The Muslim Brotherhood could be called "the mother of all Islamist organizations". It has produced many influential Islamist thinkers, including its founder, Hassan al-Bannah, and the Islamist ideologue Sayyid Qutb; it has also been the model for many other Islamist organizations, including Hizbut Tahrir and Hamas. The main difference between the Brotherhood and more radical groups like al Qaeda and ISIS is that it is willing to participate in existing political systems and to operate as a non-violent political party. This approach was highly successful following the populists uprisings dubbed the 'Arab Spring', when the Muslim Brotherhood leader Muhammad Morsi was elected president of Egypt in 2012. However, the Egyptian military cracked down on the Brotherhood a year later, deposing Morsi and killing or imprisoning thousands of Brotherhood members. This has driven the group back underground, radicalizing its members and driving some of them to more militant groups like ISIS.

It is worth noting that the founder of the Muslim Brotherhood, Hassan al-Banna, was actually a Freemason at one time, and received initiation into a Sufi (Islamic mystical) order. The Brotherhood allied itself with and emulated the Nazi party in the 1930s, and also received support from the CIA against Arab nationalists in the 1950s and 60s. These facts, along with its willingness to participate in democratic systems that aren't part of Islamic tradition, has made the Brotherhood highly suspect in the eyes of many Wahhabis and Salafis.

Muslim World League

The *Muslim World League* (MWL) is an organization based in Mecca, Saudi Arabia, that is dedicated to propagating the Wahhabist version of Islam around the world. Founded in 1962, the organization funds the construction of mosques, distribution of Qurans, charity work, *Dawah* (preaching), and the publication of Islamic books. The League's stated objectives are:

- Formation of Islamic public opinion regarding the various issues of concern to Muslims, within the guidance of the Holy Qur'an and the Sunnah
- Combating ideological incursions and aberrant thought.
- Advocating the freedom of preaching to the path of God.
- Striving to protect Mosques and Mosque properties against attack.
- Preserving Islamic endowments.
- Defending the rights of the Muslim minorities.

The MWL sponsors the *General Islamic Conference*, an annual gathering of scholars and preachers who discuss important issues and set the agenda for the Saudi-aligned Muslim world. An MWL subsidiary called the *Islamic Fiqh Council* issues rulings on important matters of Islamic law.

At the Fiqh Council's first meeting in 1978, their first ruling was called "The First Resolution on Freemasonry and Affiliation with It", in which they condemned the Freemasons as a subversive, un-Islamic, pro-Zionist organization. The Resolution is important enough that we have reproduced it *Appendix B.* It is telling that the first ruling of one of the world's leading Islamic organizations was an ideological attack on Freemasonry – and by extension on the Illuminati and their New World Order project. This Resolution should be studied carefully to understand some of the key points of disagreement between Islam and the Illuminati. It is a good a summary of the roots of the conflict, and a declaration of ideological war by Islamists on one of their greatest enemies.

Not surprisingly, in view of such rulings, the MWL has been the target of numerous investigations and accusations regarding its association with Islamist terrorism and radicalism. Osama bin Laden identified the League as a primary source of funding for al Qaeda in 1993. The current leader of al Qaeda, Ayman al-Zawahiri, worked for a subsidiary of the organization at one time. Numerous financial transactions in support of Islamist groups have been traced back to MWL or its subsidiaries. It should be noted, however, that many MWL speakers have criticized the radical version of Islam espoused by ISIS and al Qaeda.

The Muslim World League is clearly an important player in the Islamist elite, propagating Saudi-centric Wahhabist Islam worldwide. Whether the Saudi elite aspire to be the leaders of a Caliphate themselves is unclear, but certainly they are threatened by the radical ISIS Caliphate on their borders, and have an interest in promoting a more moderate version of Wahabbism to defuse the threat.

Al Qaeda

Al Qaeda ("The Foundation"), founded by Osama bin Laden, Abdullah Azzam, and other Arab veterans of the Afghan jihad in 1989, represents a move beyond Muslim Brotherhood or Muslim World League-style Islamism to radical global jihadism. After their successful jihad against the Soviet Union, the al Qaeda founders decided the time was right to take on the only remaining superpower, the United States, and to topple the apostate regimes in the Muslim world. So al Qaeda became a new kind of transnational Islamist force that would wage war upon the "far enemy" (the West) as well as the "near enemy" (governments in the Muslim world). Al Qaeda aimed to be Sayyid Qutb's "Islamic vanguard" (see below): an elite army of holy warriors "marching through the vast ocean of Jahiliyya which has encompassed the entire world." They opened franchises across the world, carrying out terrorist attacks and military operations that continue to this day. Their ultimate goal was to liberate Muslim lands from infidel influence and establish a new Caliphate.

Al Qaeda became the most hunted terrorists in the world following a series of major terrorist attacks on American targets in the late 1990s, culminating in the devastating September 11th, 2001 attacks. Despite being decimated repeatedly in the wake of 9/11 and America's "War on Terror", the organization has shown an impressive ability to rebound, regroup and re-emerge wherever conditions are ripe. In the 1980s and 90s, that was Afghanistan; in the 2000s, it was Iraq; today it is Yemen, Syria, Somalia and Libya. The killing of Osama bin Laden, Anwar al-Awlaki, and other charismatic leaders hasn't stopped them; in recent years they have expanded into North Africa and India, taken over towns in Yemen, Libya and Somalia, and conducted a number of successful operations. Their most notorious recent attack was the gunning down of 11 people at the offices of the *Charlie Hebdo* newspaper in Paris in 2015. The attack was the work of two men from Al Qaeda in Yemen, who were avenging the publication of what they considered to be blasphemous cartoons mocking the prophet Muhammad.

Al Qaeda has no doubt been the most important jihadist organization of modern times. Wherever the ideology of global jihadism has strong appeal, al Qaeda remains a force to be reckoned with. Defeating al Qaeda requires defeating the ideas and vision they fight for, which thus far, the West and its 'New World Order' have been unable to do. It may be that the force that will defeat al Qaeda is not a Western military, but a more aggressive Islamist organization that makes them obsolete by accomplishing their goals – an organization such as ISIS.

Islamist Ideologues
Sayyid Qutb

One of the key ideological architects of global jihadism was an Egyptian intellectual named Sayyid Qutb. Qutb wrote a number of scholarly and political books about Islam, and was an influential member of the Muslim Brotherhood until he was executed by the Egyptian government in 1966 for his subversive activities. Qutb actually lived in the United States for two years in the late 1940s, which provoked his revulsion at the materialism, secularism, sensualism and superficiality of the American way of life.

One of Qutb's core ideas was that the modern Muslim world lived in a state of *Jahiliyya* (pre-Islamic ignorance of divine guidance). The influence of the West, the domination of Muslim lands by Westernized puppet rulers, and the decadence of Muslims themselves created a situation where Muslims were abandoning their own religious tradition in favor of the materialistic, democratic Western way of life.

Qutb's book "Milestones", published in 1964, was a call for the revitalization of Islam that laid the ideological foundation for modern global jihadism. In the book, Qutb rejected the secular, democratic systems of the West as systems of arbitrary "man-made law", as opposed to the eternal, divine law of Sharia laid down in the Quran. To Qutb, non-Islamic societies imposed tyranny upon their citizens, because they forced them to submit to the rule of other men – monarchs, dictators and demagogues – rather than freeing them to live under the unchanging justice of Islam. The role of jihad was to free humanity from these tyrannical systems of man-made law, and to remove all obstacles to the implementation of Sharia. Thus, Qutb turns Islam, which had been conservative for centuries, into *Islamism* – a militant "liberation" movement to overthrow secularized governments and install Islamic government throughout the Muslim and non-Muslim world. Qutb's Islamism thus joins International Socialism, Neoliberal Capitalism, Illuminism and Fascism as an aggressive political ideology out to conquer and remake the world.

As we shall see, Qutb's ideology is diametrically opposed to the ideology of the Illuminati. Where the Illuminati seeks to separate government from religion, Islam seeks to unite them. Where Qutb sees Western history as a process of degeneration away from religious civilization to an animal-like state of materialism, the Illuminati sees it as a grand story of human progress, enlightenment and liberation from religious barbarism. Where the Illuminati calls the Westernization of the Muslim world "progress", Qutb calls it regression to Jahiliyya.

In one important respect Qutb's ideas are similar to Illuminati ideology: his belief in the need for an Islamic "vanguard" – a militant elite who will lead the global jihad to revitalize Islam and liberate the world from secular man-made laws. As Qutb put it: "It is necessary that there should be a vanguard which sets out with this determination and then keeps walking on the path, marching through the vast ocean of Jahiliyya which has encompassed the entire world." Qutb has been criticized by many Salafis for adopting a Western mentality of revolutionary 'vanguardism', inspired by the Communist and Fascist movements of his time. Nevertheless, Qutb's ideas would become very influential on Osama bin Laden, Ayman al Zawahiri (current head of al Qaeda) and many other Salafi jihadists, who clearly see themselves as the global Islamic vanguard. Thus Qutb could be thought of as a founder of an "Islamist Illuminati", who, like Illuminati founder Adam Weishaupt, believed in the need for an elite who could operate ruthlessly, subversively and globally to bring about its new world order, and which is inspiring jihadists to do battle with the soldiers of the Western Illuminati on battlefields around the world to this day.

Abu Musab al-Siri

Another thinker who has been highly influential on modern jihadists is a Syrian with the *nom de guerre* of *Abu Musab al-Siri* (birth name Mustafa Setmariam Nasar). Like Qutb, al-Siri considered the modern world order to be completely un-Islamic, and indeed Satanic, and must therefore be overthrown by all possible means. In his most influential book, "A Global Islamic Resistance Call" al-Siri lays out some strategies for defeating the 'New World Order'. One of the strategies he advocated was the creation of decentralized cells of jihadists, who could operate covertly anywhere in the world. These jihadists would operate without being part of any formal organization, thus staying under the radar of authorities. They would carry out "lone wolf attacks", and then release statements to media taking credit for the attacks under some jihadist "brand name"(e.g. "al Qaeda" or "ISIS"). This decentralized approach would spread the jihadist brand's message without giving authorities a central target to attack. Al-Siri has clearly had a significant influence upon the methodology of the modern jihadist movement, first with al Qaeda, and now with the numerous lone-wolf attacks we have seen around the world, such as the slaying of 14 people in San Bernadino, California, that have been directly inspired by the emergence of ISIS and their Islamic Caliphate.

Osama bin Laden

Osama bin Laden is the man who, more than any other, applied the ideology of Qutb and the Salafis and brought global jihadism to the attention of the world. Born to a wealthy Saudi family, bin Laden became one of the financiers and leaders of global jihadism following his experience in the Afghan jihad against the Soviets. There, he made contact with other jihadist ideologues such as Abdullah Azzam and Ayman al-Zawahiri and formed the *al Qaeda* jihadist network.

Bin Laden released a series of *fatwas* (religious rulings) announcing his grievances and intentions. His 1996 fatwa "Declaration of War against the Americans Occupying the Land of the Two Holy Places" attacks the "Zionist-Crusader alliance" and cites the occupation of the two Holy Places (Mecca and Medina) by infidel troops as grounds for war. Bin Laden also condemns the Illuminist tactics of the Saudi media:

> The state of the press and the media which became a tool of truth-hiding and misinformation; the media carried out the plan of the enemy of idolising cult of certain personalities and spreading scandals among the believers to repel the people away from their religion.

He also warns against the divide-and-conquer tactics of the 'Zionist-Crusader' occupiers in Arabia, and claims that

> The existence of such a large country with its huge resources under the leadership of the forthcoming Islamic State, by Allah's Grace, represent a serious danger to the very existence of the Zionist state in Palestine.

Clearly bin Laden's greater vision, like that of ISIS today, was the establishment of a militant Islamic State that controls the holy places and vast resources of the Arabian peninsula, which could remake the region and expel the Zionists and Crusaders from Muslim lands.

In a 1998 fatwa called "Text of Fatwah Urging Jihad

Against Americans", bin Laden stated that "The ruling to kill the Americans and their allies – civilians and military – is an individual duty for every Muslim who can do it in any country in which it is possible to do it." He justifies this with Quranic injunctions such as "fight the pagans all together as they fight you all together." Since American sanctions and wars in Iraq had resulted in the deaths of thousands of Iraqi civilians, bin Laden reasoned that attacking Americans in kind was justified. This radical ruling was criticized by many Muslim scholars, but three years later it would be made good on with deadly effect, and continues to be the policy of al Qaeda and their even more radical offspring, ISIS.

Bin Laden's most infamous achievement was of course the 9/11 attacks on the Twin Towers and the Pentagon, a potent symbolic blow against two power centers of the New World Order. Bin Laden was also the father of al Qaeda in Iraq, which became ISIS, and he is still revered by that organization despite their falling out with al Qaeda. Overall, we can say that bin Laden is a kind of George Washington or Adam Weishaupt of the global jihad movement – an inspirational figurehead as well as a victorious commander, whose actions, more than any other single individual's, have brought the dawn of a new era of world war between the forces of Islamism and the Illuminati.

Anwar Al-Awlaki

Anwar al-Awlaki has been called "the most dangerous ideologue in the world" because he represents a new generation of Islamists, with a charismatic presence and native familiarity with Western language, culture and media. He could also be called the "American bin Laden", because of their shared Yemeni roots, global jihadist ideologies and ability to inspire followers worldwide to put their Islamist principles into militant action.

Awlaki was a prolific user of social media; he released numerous popular youtube videos discussing all aspects of Islam. A gifted story-teller, he brought the lives of Muhammad and the Sahaba vividly to life and propagated the grand narratives of Islam and jihad. In 2010, he released a video in which he praises the Islamic State of Iraq, and another in which he calls upon Muslims to kill Americans. So dangerous was Al-Awlaki by then that he became the first U.S. citizen to be assassinated by drone strike, in 2011.

Awlaki's influence on global jihadists has been immense: he created Al Qaeda's *Inspire* magazine; corresponded with and inspired the Fort Hood shooter Hasan and the "Underwear Bomber" Abdulmutallab; inspired numerous other convicted terrorists and militants; ISIS even named one of their training camps in his honor.

THE CALIPHATE

The *Caliphate*, or *Khilafa*, is the Islamic Empire: the entire global community of Muslims united behind one ruler, called the *Caliph*. The Caliphate is the central project of ISIS, whose significance must be understood if one is to grasp why ISIS fights, and what kind of world order is wants to create.

History

The Caliphate has existed for most of Islamic history in some form. It was first established immediately after the death of Muhammad in 632, when Abu Bakr was chosen by the Muslim community to be the Caliph. The word "Caliph" itself means "substitute"; the Caliph's role is to substitute for the Prophet as the leader of all Muslims. The first four Caliphs, Abu Bakr, Umar, Uthman and Ali, are called the *Rashidun* ("Rightly Guided") Caliphs; they are greatly revered as the noblest leaders of the Muslims, who established the original Islamic state, greatly expanded its borders and developed its legal and economic system. For Salafists like ISIS, the Rashidun Caliphs are the best model to be followed; after them, the Caliphates were degraded by schisms, divisions, corruption and failure to fully implement Sharia, culminating in the non-Arab Ottoman Caliphate, widely viewed by Salafis as a decadent regime that betrayed Islam and allowed the Caliphate to be toppled.

In 1924, following their loss in World War I, the Ottoman Empire collapsed and their Caliphate was abolished. This was achieved with the cooperation of the British and French imperial powers, who divided up the Middle East, redrew the borders of Iraq, Syria, Palestine and other Muslim lands according to the *Sykes-Picot Agreement*, and installed Western-friendly governments. To many in the West, this was the death blow in their long struggle against Islam. As British General Allenby said after entering Jerusalem: "Now the Crusades have ended."

From the perspective of Islamists, the abolition of the Caliphate was a catastrophe that has led to nearly a century of humiliation and colonization. Lacking a central authority that could command a united Muslim army to expel the "Crusaders and Zionists", the Muslim world has grown ever more corrupted and controlled by Western governments, values and institutions. However, the re-emergence of jihad as a potent threat in the late 20th century, the toppling of a number of non-Islamic governments during the Arab Spring, and the chaos created by the U.S. Invasion of Iraq and the Syrian civil war, has created a golden opportunity for the Islamists to reclaim their lands and re-establish their Caliphate.

The ISIS Caliphate

Recognizing their historic opportunity, ISIS seized large portions of Iraq and Syria in 2014 and declared the re-establishment of the Caliphate on the first day of Ramadan, June 29th. An Iraqi scholar named Abu Bakr al-Baghdadi announced that he was the new Caliph of the Islamic State, declared the dawn of a new era of Muslim might and called for the eruption of "volacanos of jihad".

The announcement was ideologically precise. Baghdadi fits the requirements of a Caliph, being a Muslim male descendant of the Qurayshi tribe of Muhammad, with strong moral character and authority. He is also named after *Abu Bakr*, the first Caliph after Muhammad, who united the Arabs behind Islam and began the wars of conquest to expand the religion to other lands. The name is surely no accident, since this is precisely what ISIS is seeking to do: unite the Muslim world behind their jihad, and begin to expand the borders of Islam into the jahiliyya states of the Muslim world, into Africa, Europe, Asia and the rest of the world. So, for the first time in five hundred years, Islam has a Caliphate located in the heart of the Muslim world, led by a Qurayshi Arab and dedicated to expansion of Islam by jihad. The ISIS Caliphate represents a historic triumph for the Salafi/Wahhabi brand of Islam, since it marks a return to the austere, militant, explosive *Ummah* (Muslim community) of the Rashidun Caliphs and Companions of the Prophet.

It should be noted that this Caliphate is not accepted by most mainstream Muslim scholars. A would-be Caliph is traditionally supposed to consult with scholars and get the approval of the wider Muslim community. ISIS simply seized territory by force and declared themselves the Caliphate, abrogating all other Islamic authorities. Even a large portion of the jihadist community, including its rival al Qaeda, has rejected ISIS's Caliphate for its extreme aggressiveness and ambition. Having said that, ISIS does enjoy significant popular support within the Muslim world – up to 15% according to some polls, with up to 30% undecided. This means there are potentially hundreds of millions of ISIS supporters around the Muslim world. The fate of their nascent Caliphate may hinge on whether ISIS can continue to win on the battlefield and expand in the face of massive global opposition, and thereby demonstrate to believers that Allah is on their side.

The First Statement of the Caliph

ISIS Caliph Abu Bakr Al-Baghdadi

On August 1, 2014, Caliph Al-Baghdadi released a statement to the world, announcing the establishment of the Islamic State and calling upon Muslims worldwide to support it:

> So let the world know that we are living today in a new era. Whoever was heedless must now be alert. Whoever was sleeping must now awaken. Whoever was shocked and amazed must comprehend. The Muslims today have a loud, thundering statement, and possess heavy boots. They have a statement that will cause the world to hear and understand the meaning of terrorism, and boots that will trample the idol of nationalism, destroy the idol of democracy and uncover its deviant nature.

> So listen, O ummah of Islam. Listen and comprehend.

Stand up and rise. For the time has come for you to free yourself from the shackles of weakness, and stand in the face of tyranny, against the treacherous rulers – the agents of the crusaders and the atheists, and the guards of the jews.

O ummah of Islam, indeed the world today has been divided into two camps and two trenches, with no third camp present: The camp of Islam and faith, and the camp of kufr (disbelief) and hypocrisy – the camp of the Muslims and the mujahidin everywhere, and the camp of the jews, the crusaders, their allies, and with them the rest of the nations and religions of kufr, all being led by America and Russia, and being mobilized by the jews.

Here we see clearly that ISIS views the world as being divided into two warring camps: the camp of Islam and the camp of disbelief. When al-Baghdadi speaks of the latter – the "agents of the crusaders and the atheists, and the guards of the jews" – he is speaking of the West, and its Christian, secularist and Zionist ideologies – the three ideologies that are at the heart of the "New World Order" project we shall discuss later.

Al-Baghdadi then attacks the Western powers for their plundering of Muslim lands, their installation of puppet rulers, and their promotion of un-Islamic ideologies:

Indeed the Muslims were defeated after the fall of their khilāfah (caliphate). Then their state ceased to exist, so the disbelievers were able to weaken and humiliate the Muslims, dominate them in every region, plunder their wealth and resources, and rob them of their rights. They accomplished this by attacking and occupying their lands, placing their treacherous agents in power to rule the Muslims with an iron fist, and spreading dazzling and deceptive slogans such as: civilization, peace, co-existence, freedom, democracy, secularism, baathism, nationalism, and patriotism, among other false slogans.

Al-Baghdadi goes on to recite a litany of crimes committed by the 'global forces of disbelief' against Muslims, which he mocks by saying sarcastically: "All this is not terrorism. Rather it is freedom, democracy, peace, security, and tolerance!"

Al-Baghdadi makes it clear that the Caliphate intends to establish an alternative world order, which will be open to all peoples, of every race and region across the globe:

O Muslims everywhere, glad tidings to you and expect good. Raise your head high, for today – by Allah's grace – you have a state and khilāfah, which will return your dignity, might, rights, and leadership. It is a state where the Arab and non-Arab, the white man and black man, the easterner and westerner are all brothers. It is a khilāfah that gathered the Caucasian, Indian, Chinese, Shāmī, Iraqi, Yemeni, Egyptian, Maghribī (North African), American, French, German, and Australian. Allah brought their hearts together, and thus, they became brothers by His grace, loving each other for the sake of Allah, standing in a single trench, defending and guarding each other, and sacrificing themselves for one another. Their blood mixed and became one, under a single flag and goal, in one pavilion, enjoying this blessing, the blessing of faithful brotherhood. If kings were to taste this blessing, they would abandon their kingdoms and fight over this grace. So all praise and thanks are due to Allah.

In other words, the Islamic State's project is an another form of radical globalism, which, like the Illuminati's New World Order, seeks to erase the old divisions of tribe and nationality and unite all mankind under one ideology and one global government – the Caliphate. Al-Baghdadi's final statement makes the Caliphate's goal of world domination very clear:

> This is my advice to you. If you hold to it, you will conquer Rome and own the world, if Allah wills.

Theological Significance

To the followers of ISIS, the re-establishment of the Caliphate is a monumental event, with vast theological significance. It activates Islamic laws and obligations that aren't valid in the absence of the Caliphate, and makes Islam potentially a much more potent force in the world.
For one, all Muslims are expected to give their allegiance to a Caliphate. In a reliable hadith, Muhammad said:

> "Whoever dies without being bound by the oath of allegiance (bay`ah), dies the death of the time of ignorance (Jahillyya)."

Here bay'ah refers to the traditional oath of allegiance Muslims are to take to their rightful leader – whether that be a tribal sheikh, monarch or Caliph. This hadith has been interpreted by ISIS supporters to mean that Muslims who don't take an oath to Caliph al-Baghdadi will die a death of disbelief, and are therefore condemning themselves to eternal Hellfire. This has been a powerful recruiting tool for ISIS, even for those who can't migrate to the lands of the

Caliphate. A number of jihadists have recorded their oaths to Baghdadi before conducting their attacks in the West, including the San Bernardino attackers who gunned down 14 people.

Additionally, the advent of a Caliphate enables the full enactment of Sharia, which includes its punishments (*hudud*), social welfare policies, taxation and ideology of warfare. Thus we have seen the implementation of harsh hudud such as amputations of the hands of thieves, beheadings of apostates and stonings of adulterers in ISIS-controlled territory. What is less publicised are the social welfare policies of the Islamic State, which include free health care, food and welfare payments. More ominously, the advent of the Caliphate empowers the Caliph to wage not just defensive jihad against invaders of Muslim lands, but to engage in offensive jihad to harass the *kuffar* (disbelievers) and conquer more territory for the Caliphate, without requiring a pretext of defense. In ISIS's view, any land which is preventing Sharia from being implemented is in the *Dar al-Harb (House of War)*, and is a legitimate target for attack.

ISIS STRATEGY

What strategies, tactics and principles is ISIS employing in their war to defeat the New World Order and establish their Caliphate? Let us look at some of the key ones below.

The Management of Savagery

A central strategy being used by ISIS is what we'll call the *"Management of Savagery"* or *"MOS"* model. The MOS model was described in the electronic book *"The Management of Savagery: The Most Critical Stage Through Which the Umma Will Pass,"* written by Islamist strategist Abu Bakr Naji and distributed on the internet in 2004. The MOS model is Naji's strategy for defeating superpowers – particularly America and its allies – in the Muslim world, based on Islamists' previous experience fighting the Soviet Union and America. MOS is based on the idea that Muslim civilization, having experienced centuries of decline and the abolition of its Caliphate in 1924, has entered a stage Naji calls the "administrations of savagery." In this stage, formerly great powers have been divided into smaller, weaker states whose governments, being too weak to maintain order, have fallen into a state of subservience to Western power and ideas. Islamists believe they have a religious duty to end this situation by overthrowing Westernized regimes in the Muslim world, and attacking America and the West directly.

Maji defines three primary goals of the MOS strategy to defeat America:

- Destroy America's reputation and increase the confidence of Muslims. Do this by discrediting the superpower's "deceptive media halo" of invincibility, and by drawing it into direct conflict with jihadists in Muslim lands. This will create sympathy in the population and make them realize that they are capable of resisting America if they depose America-friendly regimes.
- Increase recruitment to the jihad by carrying out dazzling operations against America and capitalizing on resentment over direct American intervention in the Muslim world.
- Expose the weakness of America's centralized power and distance from Muslim lands. Force America to fight directly instead of by proxy and in the media, thus demonstrating to non-Islamists, including Americans, that it is incapable of maintaining order in distant lands.

This strategy was summarized by one analyst this way:

> Al-Naji's doctrine, drawn from the Afghan experience, is based on a simple formula: enrage the United States so that it oversteps local security forces and engages directly with local jihadis, which in turn incites other Muslims to join the fight against the "occupying" power, thereby increasing al-Qaeda's strength and prestige. The strategy assumes that local Muslims will have much greater staying power than the United States because they can fight

so much more cheaply and have a greater tolerance for casualties.

This strategy would explain al Qaeda attacks going back to the U.S.S. Cole bombing in 2000 and 9/11/2001. The U.S.-led invasions of Afghanistan and Iraq, which bogged down and created widespread sympathy for the militants, played into the jihadists' hands. The MOS strategy also explains why ISIS is taking superpower provocation to a new level of sophistication in Iraq and Syria, and is conducting 'dazzling operations' in the streets of Europe.

The Logic of Terror

In *The Management of Savagery*, Abu Bakr Naji makes the following chilling claim:

> "We are now in circumstances resembling the circumstances after the death of the Messenger (peace and blessings be upon him) and the outbreak of apostasy or the like of that which the believers faced in the beginning of the jihad. Thus, we need to massacre (others) and (to take) actions like those that were undertaken against the Banu Qurayza and their like."

Naji recommends polarizing the society this way:

> "dragging the masses into the battle requires more actions which will inflame opposition and which will make the people enter into the battle, willing or unwilling, such that each individual will go to the side which he supports. We must make this battle very violent, such that death is a heartbeat away."

Naji further suggests that jihadists should demoralize their enemies by pursuing a "paying the price" policy of punishing their enemies whenever they are attacked, never relenting, and attacking from many locations. He uses this policy to justify hostage taking, saying: "The policy of violence must also be followed such that if the demands are not met, the hostages should be liquidated in a terrifying manner, which will send fear into the hearts of the enemy and his supporters." Here we have a chilling strategic explanation for the kidnappings and public beheading of hostages James Foley, Steven Sotloff and others following unheeded warnings to America to stop their bombing campaign against ISIS.

Analyst Alistair Crooke described the strategic nature of ISIS terrorism this way:

> "In sum, *the beheadings and other violence practiced by ISIS are not some whimsical, crazed fanaticism, but a very deliberate, considered strategy.* The military strategy pursued by ISIS in Iraq, too, is neither spontaneous nor some populist adventure, but rather reflects very professional well-prepared military planning.
>
> The seemingly random violence has a precise purpose: Its aim is to strike huge fear; to break the psychology of a people -- and, according to reports, this is exactly what *Da'ish* has already succeeded in doing for many of the residents of Baghdad."

Crooke claims that ISIS operations such as seizing fuel supplies and dams are done intentionally to polarize civilian populations. This is consistent with Naji's repeated calls for the tactic of polarization in MOS, about which he says: "By polarization here, I mean dragging the masses into the battle

such that polarization is created between all of the people."
According to Naji, this will allow jihadists to draw people to
their cause who will play a decisive role in their battles. This
polarization tactic would explain much of the brutality
reportedly committed by ISIS forces against civilians: as a
conquering army, the more they polarize populations, the
more they can attract friends, eliminate foes and perpetuate
the conditions of war in which they thrive.

The Return of the Gold Dinar

Another strategy the Islamic State is pursuing to break
the dominant power of the Western world order is to
establish its own currency and financial system, totally
independent of the dollar-centric global system. ISIS currency
will follow the traditional Islamic system of being
denominated in gold, silver and copper. This is in contrast the
American dollar, which since 1971 has been a *fiat currency*,
meaning that it is no longer convertible into gold or any other
fixed asset.

In a video called "The Return of the Gold Dinar", ISIS
shows gold, silver and copper coins being minted, modelled
on the *dinars* of the early Caliphates. The video explains that
the dinars will be part of a new Islamic financial system which
forbids usury (collection of interest), in accordance with
Islamic law. Thus, in addition to the ideological, military and
cultural dimensions of its struggle, ISIS is putting itself into
direct financial conflict with the New World Order as well.
Indeed, the narrator claims in the video that the new currency
will deliver a "second blow" (after 9/11) to the American
"capitalist financial system of enslavement", which will "mark
the death of this oppressive bank note and bring America, the
symbol of injustice and tyranny, to her knees." While there is
little evidence that this currency is actually in use in ISIS-

controlled territory, if nothing else the threat is another weapon in the Islamists' ideological and propaganda war against the Illuminati.

WHO IS THE ILLUMINATI?

Now let us turn our attention to the other side of this "clash of civilizations", and ask: who is really behind the "New World Order" project that many Muslims see as their main enemy? What is the hidden power behind modern Western civilization that has turned it into the unreligious, anti-Islamic, perhaps even Satanic force that it is today? The main culprit is a shadowy association we shall call *the Illuminati*.

Myth or Masters of Deception?

The "Illuminati" is a meme that is clouded in myth, disinformation, confusion and conspiracy theory. Many deny that it ever existed, or claim that it is long-dead. Others believe it is part of a vast, ancient occult conspiracy, involving bloodlines of 13 powerful families that trace their origins to ancient Babylon, or even to an alien reptilian race. Others claim to be part of an Illuminati movement that is recruiting the masses and openly propagating a "one world religion" and a "New World Order." One can easily get lost in a rather crazy world when investigating this elusive organization. In what follows, I will take a "middle way" by discussing verifiable historical organizations and events that have been associated with the Illuminati, while speculating at times about the possibility of more outlandish conspiracies. I will neither buy into the wilder theories nor automatically dismiss them. Like all subjects outside the accepted narratives where all the facts aren't available, the Illuminati requires us to use our intuition to fill in the gaps in the story. For reasons that will become clear, we are on the trail of an organization that *doesn't want to be found.*

The Illuminati Defined

The *Illuminati*, broadly speaking, refers to all esoteric (secretive) organizations with similar ideologies to Adam Weishaupt's original *Bavarian Illuminati* group, and which have had a powerful influence on Western civilization and the world since the late 18th century. Illuminati organizations can be divided into several overlapping categories or camps; the four we will focus on are the *Enlightenment Illuminati,* the *Luciferians,* the *Synarchists* and the *Zionists.*

Note that the Illuminati should be distinguished from the high plutocracy – the class of extremely wealthy families who control a large percentage of the world's wealth and power, such as the Rockefellers and the Rothschilds. This group is highly influential, but may not hold to any ideology or vision beyond maintaining their wealth and power. What distinguishes true Illuminati from mere plutocratic schemers is their belief in a vision of society, grand ideals and a new world order they wish to create. The Illuminati is like a high priesthood, who have many sponsors among the money and power elite, but are themselves devoted primarily to ideas.

The Bavarian Illuminati

The term *Illuminati* originated with a group called the *Bavarian Illuminati* – a German secret society founded in 1776 by a law professor named Adam Weishaupt. Weishaupt, born of Jewish parents, was educated by Jesuits but broke with the Church following their banning of the Jesuit order in 1773.

Reliable information about Weishaupt's influences is difficult to obtain, but allegedly he was initiated into the Freemasons around 1774, and came under the influence of a mysterious occultist named Kolmer, who taught him secret doctrines originating in ancient Egypt and Persia. Other possible influences on Weishaupt include the Knights Templar (see below), the Lurianic Kabbalists and the *Alumbrados* ("the Illuminated"), a heretical 16th century Spanish sect of Gnostic Christians who believed that the human spirit can attain perfection such that sin is permissible and direct knowledge of God outside of religion is possible. But the main ideological influence on Weishaupt appears to be Masonic and Enlightenment ideals, as expressed in statements like this:

> Man is not bad except as he is made so by arbitrary morality. He is bad because religion, the state, and bad examples pervert him. When at last reason becomes the religion of men, then will the problem be solved.

Here we have a clear statement of the Illuminati's "religion of reason", which put them in direct conflict with the teachings of the Catholic Church in Weishaupt's time, as it does with the teachings of Islam today.

A key point about Weishaupt's Illuminati is that while they espoused open, rationalist ideals, they operated in secret among an elite, and had an ambitious power agenda. The organization was structured like a pyramid, with each member having two members below him, allowing them to propagate their directives widely from the top down. Weishaupt is credited with this statement:

I have two immediately below me into whom I breathe my whole spirit, and each of these two has again two others, and so on. In this way I can set a thousand men in motion and on fire in the simplest manner, and in this way one must impart orders and operate on politics.

A book from 1798 called *Proofs of a Conpiracy Against All the Religions and Governments of Europe Carried on in the Secret Meetings of the Free Masons, Illuminati, and Reading Societies* claimed to expose the Illuminati's agenda by publishing some of Weishaupt's letters. There, Weishaupt is quoted as saying "the great strength of our Order lies in its concealment"; he discusses the adoption of many forms such as Freemasonry, schemes to influence libraries and reading societies so as to "turn the public mind which way we will", and to "try to obtain an influence in ... all offices which have any effect, either in forming, or in managing, or even in directing the mind of man." Weishaupt also wrote:

> Do you realize sufficiently what it means to rule—to rule in a secret society? Not only over the lesser or more important of the populace, but over the best of men, over men of all ranks, nations, and religions, to rule without external force, to unite them indissolubly, to breathe one spirit and soul into them, men distributed over all parts of the world?

While this may sound like far-fetched vision, anyone who can perceive the degree of occult manipulation of public opinion and politics that goes on in Western society to this day would not be unjustified in concluding that Weishaupt's scheme was wildly successful, and the heirs of his Illuminati rule over us today.

Weishaupt's influence on world history has surely been immense, though still largely unknown. Thomas Jefferson and French revolutionaries wrote admiringly of him; the Freemasons adopted many of his ideas; the revolutions in America and France owe debts to him; the religious and monarchical establishment of Europe warned against him and sought to shut him down. It may be no exaggeration to say that the occult war Weishaupt launched against the Church and the monarchies of Europe achieved total victory, and the war on Islam is the latest round of an ongoing "global jihad" to establish the Illuminati's "religion of reason" across the world.

Roots of the Illuminati

It is difficult to determine how far back the origins of the Illuminati go. Some trace them back to ancient Babylon, Egypt or Sumeria, or even to ancient aliens, but we will not go that far back in this book. Our story begins in medieval Europe, with a group called the *Knights Templar*.

The Knights Templar

The Knights Templar were an order of Christian knights that formed in the 12th century to defend pilgrims from Muslim attacks in the Holy Land. After the Crusaders' conquest of Jerusalem in 1099, the Templars established their headquarters at the al-Aqsa mosque on the Temple Mount. The Order's size and power grew rapidly: they built the first modern financial system, spanning all of Christendom, acquired vast wealth and developed a standing army that served as the shock troops of the Crusades. The Knights Templar were a "state within a state", a multinational corporation, an army of holy warriors, and the nexus of a

"Crusader State" called *Outremer*. In many ways, they were the al Qaeda or ISIS of their time!

With their great wealth and power, the Templars inevitably became arrogant and corrupt – allegedly disobeying kings and popes, delving for occult secrets amid the ruins of the Temple Mount, incorporating practices of the Muslim Assassins, Jewish Kabbalists and even Satanists. According to Church Inquisitors, the Templars' practices included the desecration of religious symbols, pagan and Satanic idolatry, sexual perversion and black magic rituals. This brought a crackdown by both the Church and the monarchy: on "Friday the 13th", 1307 in Paris, many Templars were arrested, imprisoned and executed, and the Order's last Grand Master, Jacques de Molay, was burned at the stake. As we shall see, these events are still significant today, as terrorist attacks echo the attack on the Knights Templar more than 700 years ago.

After the crackdown in 1307, the Templars were driven underground and into exile. To escape persecution, some relocated to Scotland and infiltrated the stone mason guilds, which were influential civil societies at the time. Others relocated to Switzerland and helped found that secretive banking nation; still others joined knightly orders in Spain, Germany and France to escape the Inquisition. Then the Templars disappear from history for several centuries, and their fate becomes highly speculative. One theory is that they continued their lineage of Grand Masters in secret, plotting their revenge upon the papacy and the monarchy, and infiltrating various organizations such as the Freemasons in preparation for their return to power.

Some of the titles of higher ranking Scottish Rite Freemasons reflect their possible Knights Templar origins, such as "Knight of the Temple" and "Knight of Jerusalem".

An interesting anecdote that suggests a connection between the Templars and the Freemasons occurred during the French Revolution (a Masonic/Illuminist coup, as we discuss later). When King Louis XVI was guillotined in a public square in Paris, an onlooker shouted: "Jacques de Molay, you have been avenged!" If the Templar-Masonic connection is real, then in fact, Molay was avenged. For the French Revolution marked the end of both the monarchy and the Church that had crushed the Templars five centuries earlier, and the beginning of the Freemasonic conquest of the West.

The Freemasons

The Freemasons are a secret society with millions of members and tens of thousands of lodges around the world. The ruling bodies of Freemasonry are called *Grand Lodges*, which govern all the Masonic lodges of a given nation or state, and are led by *Grand Masters*. Masonic lodges are clubs where members fraternize, conduct ceremonies, give lectures and initiate members. Freemasonry is a hierarchical order, with degrees that can go as high as 33rd degree. Members must be invited to join, must believe in a supreme being and must keep their degree activities secret. Freemasonry claims to be compatible with almost all religions, though in effect it functions as a substitute religion, by providing social life, meaning, symbolism and hierarchy to its members.

Outwardly, Freemasonry appears to be little more than a network of social clubs with no grand ambitions or influence, but this appearance is deceiving. There is no doubt that Freemasonry has wielded immense hidden influence on societies since the 18th century, when it spearheaded the American and French Revolutions. There is also evidence that at its highest levels, the Freemasons are the descendants of

Adam Weishaupt's Illuminati. This is due to the fact that after being driven out of Bavaria, the Illuminati infiltrated the Freemasons and were able to transform them into an instrument of the Illuminati agenda. Soon, these "Illuminized" Freemasons would make contact with German financial elites – most notably the infamous Rothschild banking family. By the early 19ᵗʰ century, a nexus of Illuminati, Freemasons and German/Jewish financiers was established that has been a dominant hidden force in world affairs ever since.

The Freemasons have been opposed by organized religions since their inception. Their main enemy in Europe was the Catholic Church, who saw them as a threat to their moral authority and social control. In 1738, Pope Clement XII issued a papal bull excommunicating Freemasons as a subversive secret society of "libertines and miscreants". Many more Papal Bulls were issued against Freemasonry, including Pope Leo XIII's proclamation that it was a secret society seeking to "revive the manners and customs of the pagans" and "establish Satan's kingdom on Earth." This prohibition was confirmed as recently as 1983 and remains the official position of the Catholic Church today.

Freemasonry in the Muslim World

In the Muslim world, Freemasonry made inroads during the period of Western colonialism, establishing lodges on the Arabian peninsula, throughout North Africa, the Levant and Persia in the 19ᵗʰ and early 20ᵗʰ centuries. These lodges have since been almost all extinguished, due to anti-colonial revolutions, Islamic revivals and reactions to the presence of the strongly Masonic state of Israel. In Iran, for example, Freemasonry once had a Grand Lodge with a large membership, but during the Islamic Revolution their Temples were raided, their property seized, many members were executed or exiled, and the Lodge was completely destroyed. In Egypt, home of one of the oldest and largest Masonic presences in the Muslim world, all Lodges were shut down by the nationalist Nasser following the Suez War of 1956 and the execution of Israeli master spy and Mason, Eli Cohen, in 1964. In 1978, the Islamic Fiqh Council released the ten-point condemnation of Freemasonry discussed earlier (see Appendix A). Freemasonry has been all but extinct in the region ever since.

The fall of Freemasonry in the Muslim world was accompanied by the rise of militant Islamism beginning in the late 1960s. Following the devastating defeat of Arab Nationalist forces at the hands of the Israelis in the 1967 war, there was a strong movement to revive the Islamic foundations of Arab societies, to unite the Umma and purge it of the foreign influences and puppet regimes which had brought such dishonor to the Arab world. In 1979, the Iranian Revolution and the Afghan jihad drove a wave of Islamic fundamentalism that further inflamed the Muslim world against Western influence. The expulsion of Freemasonry from Muslim lands could be seen as an opening salvo of a new great war between the forces of Islam and the forces of the Freemasonic West.

THE ENLIGHTENMENT ILLUMINATI

Adam Weishaupt's Illuminati was a founding faction of the larger *Enlightenment Illuminati* – the entire class of "enlightened", rational, "progressive" elites who claim to want to make a better world and reduce the level of ignorance, poverty, war, suffering, etc. across the globe. This Illuminati is elitist but apparently benevolent; they believe that an enlightened elite should work to bring about a liberal world order, and they have established a network of powerful global institutions to implement their goals. They employ scientists, technocrats, governmental and non-governmental organizations, think tanks and corporations globally to influence societies and promote their agenda. I call this group the "Enlightenment Illuminati", after the *Enlightenment* intellectual movement discussed in more detail later. Note that when I speak generically of the 'Illuminati', I am primarily referring to this group.

Examples of the Enlightenment Illuminati's projects include the Council on Foreign Relations, an organization of nearly 5000 members of the political, corporate, security, intellectual and media elite that has had a leading role in the Western world order since 1918. The Council was instrumental in the creation of both the League of Nations and the United Nations; their primary interests include globalization, free trade and the creation of large economic and political blocs such as NAFTA and the European Union. Similarly, the Trilateral Commission, founded by David Rockefeller, works to accelerate globalization and create close ties at the highest levels of government and business across the world. The Bilderberg Group is an annual conference of elites that promotes global free market capitalism and world government. The Club of Rome is another elite globalist think tank, famous for *The Limits to Growth,* a study which predicted a likely collapse of civilization in the 21st century if population and resource use weren't brought under control globally.

All of these groups are founded on Enlightenment Illuminati principles of secularism, rationalism, elitism and globalism; none has as any religious ideology. The basic hubris of the Enlightenment – that by his reason, technology, money and social innovations, man can engineer and "improve" the world without limits – drives all these groups to seek global domination. Thus, they inevitably come into conflict with other traditions and ideologies with different ideas about mankind's place in the world – notably Islam, which teaches an attitude of humility before God and His creation.

The Enlightenment Cult

Much of the ideology of the Illuminati has its origins in the 18th century philosophical movement called the "Enlightenment." This movement, centered in France, promoted ideals such as pragmatism, reason, capitalism and constitutional republicanism over monarchy, magical thinking, religion, theocracy and tradition. The Enlightenment would sweep through the intelligentsia of the Western world, transforming its academies, its culture and its political systems. The Illuminati can be thought of as the most Machiavellian, power-hungry and cult-like faction of the Enlightenment movement.

This Illuminati had from the outset two very powerful enemies: the Church and the Monarchy. These were the two institutions whose power the Enlightenment cult threatened most, because of its emphasis on rationalism, secularism and egalitarianism over faith and hereditary aristocracy. Because its enemies were so powerful, in its early days the cult had to operate somewhat covertly, advancing its ideas among cabals of intellectual elites rather than among the more traditionalist masses. Important early members of the Enlightenment cult included the French philosophers Voltaire, Jean-Jacques Rousseau and Denis Diderot. While they published their ideas publicly, as their threat to the established order became more serious, they faced censorship and persecution.

The cult also extended its tentacles across the Atlantic, attracting talented American elites who wanted to be part of the new European avante-garde. Benjamin Franklin made numerous trips to Europe, where he met Voltaire and other Enlightenment cult luminaries. Thomas Jefferson spent considerable time in Paris around the time of the French Revolution, and was no doubt initiated into the Illuminati cult while there. Both men incorporated Enlightenment and Illuminati ideals in the founding documents of the United States; the revolutionary creeds of "all men are created equal", "life, liberty and the pursuit of happiness" and the various rights enshrined in its Constitution are derived directly from Enlightenment philosophy.

The French Revolution which was next instigated by the Enlightenment cultists created an even bigger shockwave than the American one; it would eventually roll across Europe and topple the monarchies and Churches that had dominated

Western civilization for centuries. Thus, with the triumph of the Enlightenment, a new breed of rationalist philosophers and scientists become the ascendant priesthood in the Western world. These new Enlightenment priests wield reason, science and industry as their primary tools of power, and for the past two centuries they have been highly successful in spreading their potent and disruptive ideology across the globe.

The Globalist Agenda

The Illuminati is driven by a global agenda of world transformation, unification and centralization of power. Their agenda can be summarized by the following five goals:

- Global government
- Global market
- Global currency
- Global ideology
- Global ethnicity

By establishing these five regimes, the old divisions of nationality, economy, religion, culture and tribe can be abolished, uniting all humanity in a truly global civilization. This new order could be the "End of History", "neoliberal" regime described by Francis Fukuyama, in which the entire world has adopted secular, liberal, multicultural capitalism as the best model for all peoples. Or it could be a socialist model such as the Soviet Union, where capitalism is reigned in, decision-making is highly centralized and many freedoms are curbed. The Globalists have shown a willingness to accept both corporate capitalism and socialism, as long as their main objectives are achieved.

If we analyze the objectives of the various Illuminist

institutions, we find that they are all promoting these five goals in some way. The United Nations is the beginning of a global government; free trade agreements and economic unions are moving toward a global market; the petrodollar is a de facto global currency; the New Age and "interfaith" movements are attempts to create a global religion; the open immigration policies, multiculturalism, and global entertainment industry are attempts to create a global ethnicity.

If you investigate all of these efforts, you will find that they are sponsored, promoted and controlled by high level Illuminists. For example, the Rockefellers have long sponsored various interfaith and New Age organizations such as the World Council of Churches, the Temple of Understanding and the Esalen Institute; pro-free trade and open borders groups are funded by Illuminist financiers like George Soros; the entertainment industry is dominated by Illuminists, as shown by the prevalence of Illuminati symbolism (one eye, pyramid, devil's horns, owls, etc.) among the biggest stars; and so on. The point is, the Illuminati agenda is the opposite of a grassroots mass movement; it is top-down, elitist, and always has the effect of centralizing power in the hands of Illuminist-controlled individuals and organizations.

The Georgia Guidestones

The Georgia Guidestones are an interesting Illuminati project that spells out the group's values and agenda for all the world to see. The Guidestones are six large granite monoliths inscribed with what might be called the "ten commandments of the Illuminati", in eight major world languages:

1. Maintain humanity under 500,000,000 in perpetual

balance with nature.
2. Guide reproduction wisely — improving fitness and diversity.
3. Unite humanity with a living new language.
4. Rule passion — faith — tradition — and all things with tempered reason.
5. Protect people and nations with fair laws and just courts.
6. Let all nations rule internally resolving external disputes in a world court.
7. Avoid petty laws and useless officials.
8. Balance personal rights with social duties.
9. Prize truth — beauty — love — seeking harmony with the infinite.
10. Be not a cancer on the earth — Leave room for nature — Leave room for nature.

Here we see clearly the Illuminati's global agenda, to unite the world with a new language, guide its reproduction, drastically reduce its population, and promote various rationalist, humanist and Freemasonic values. Some of these guidelines clearly conflict with traditional monotheistic values, such as "be fruitful and multiply" and treating reproduction as something sacred. "Uniting humanity" with an invented language suggests social engineering and cultural destruction on a global scale. While many of the commandments sound reasonable, in practice it is difficult to see how they could be implemented with creating some sort of global dictatorship.

Why would such stones be constructed, at a cost of hundreds of thousands of dollars and in conditions of secrecy, and who would have the resources and vision to do so? Was their placement in the "bible belt" of the United States a deliberate provocation or act of conquest? Doesn't the fact that these stones, with their obviously Freemasonic, non-biblical commandments, were placed in the American bible belt without being destroyed suggest that the Enlightenment Illuminati has already conquered Christian civilization? Anyone who doubts the existence of an Illuminati must ask themselves these questions, and provide plausible answers!

Global Government

Among the major items on the agenda of this Illuminati are the prevention of "Climate Change", environmental sustainability, population control, the creation of super-states such as the European Union and the North American Union, World Government, the marginalization of religious institutions, and the absorption of societies worldwide into their media, educational and cultural matrix. The hallmarks of the Enlightenment Illuminati are the drive toward ever-larger structures of technocratic power and social control, and the celebration of science and rationalism over religion.

In 1992, the United Nations released an action plan called *Agenda 21*, which laid out a program for managing "sustainable development" throughout the world in order to mitigate Climate Change and other environmental problems. The Agenda has four dimensions:

Section I: Social and Economic Dimensions is concerned with combating poverty, especially in developing countries, altering consumption patterns, achieving a more sustainable population, etc.

Section II: Conservation and Management of Resources for Development addresses environment protection measures against pollution, deforestation, loss of biodiversity, radioactive waste and the management of biotechnology.

Section III: Strengthening the Role of Major Groups is concerned with making cultural changes to promote sustainability, such as education of youth and women, introduction of non-government organizations (NGOs), and giving a stronger voice to indigenous peoples and farmers.

Section IV: Means of Implementation addresses the use of science, technology, education, international institutions and financial mechanisms to promote sustainability.

This ambitious agenda, which may sound reasonable on paper, in reality requires the disruption of traditional societies and values throughout the world. It would bring global organizations into these societies that would have veto power over the local governments. These NGOs would reflect the values of the United Nations, which was founded by the West and is strongly Illuminist in its ideology. This explains why some of the most militant opposition to the U.N.'s agenda has occurred in the Muslim world, where U.N. Workers have come under attack as agents of Crusaders and Western Imperialists. The attempt by the United Nations to impose its global agenda is one of the key vectors by which the Illuminati vs. Islam war could turn hot.

Illuminati Mythology

The Enlightenment Illuminati doesn't promote a religion as such, but they do promote their mythos and worldview via popular culture. A prime example of Illuminati mythology is the popular *Star Trek* television series and movies. While far-fetched in many ways, the political and cultural vision of the series – of a liberal civilization dominated by an expansionist world government called the *Federation*, with no national or racial distinctions, no signs of any religion, and a culture that emphasizes science and rationality – looks very much like an Illuminist myth of the future they would like to create. The creator of Star Trek, Gene Roddenberry, was himself purportedly a Freemason, with close connections to elite members of the United Nations and the military. The Star Trek programs themselves were full of Illuminati symbolism, such as the pyramid/eye uniform patches, the Kabbalistic Vulcan hand salute, pyramid hand gestures, and the United Nations-like flag of the Federation. Star Trek is an example of how the Illuminati uses cultural *programming* – television, movies, books, comic books, music, etc – to propagate mythologies and visions of society that they hope will replace more traditional and religious ones.

OTHER ILLUMINATI FACTIONS

The Luciferians

The *Luciferian Illuminati* are powerful elites who have a more metaphysical motivation for creating a New World Order than the rationalist Enlightenment Illuminati. Luciferian Illuminists speak of their devotion to *Lucifer*, the "light-bringer", who they believe is the bringer of knowledge and liberation to mankind. They contrast Lucifer with *Yahweh*, the vengeful, tyrannical god of the Jews, Christians and Muslims, whose reign they wish to overthrow. We include in the Luciferian camp the elite followers of various New Age, Occult, "Gaian" and "Singularitarian" creeds, which promote the advent of global government, technologies of global control, humans evolving into supermen, eco-mysticism, ritual magic and the overthrow of the Abrahamic religions.

Notable Luciferian Illuminists include Helena Blavatsky, founder of Theosophy and mother of the New Age movement, who wrote:

> Lucifer represents life, thought, progress, civilization, liberty, independence. Lucifer is the Logos, the Serpent, the Saviour... It is Lucifer who is the God of our planet and the only God... Lucifer is the divine

and terrestrial light, the Holy Ghost and Satan at one and the same time.

Blavatsky has had tremendous influence on the world via the New Age movement, which has spread throughout the West and normalized many Eastern, pagan, and occult ideas that contradict monotheistic beliefs. Blavatsky's disciple, Alice Bailey, was another influential New Age "prophet", who promoted an ideology called "The Plan", which called for global unity ("Harmonic Convergence"), world government and world religion. As Bailey put it: "The spirit has gone out of the old faiths and the true spiritual light is transferring itself into a new form which will manifest on earth eventually as the new world religion." In 1922, Bailey founded an organization called the *Lucis Trust,* which has been influential in guiding the United Nations toward the fulfilment of 'The Plan' ever since. Numerous elite individuals and organizations, including John D. Rockefeller, industrialist Maurice Strong, UN assistant Secretary General Robert Muller, Al Gore, Mikhail Gorbachev, the Bilderbergers, Planetary Citizens and the Club of Rome, have expressed sympathy with Bailey's new globalist religion.

Some prominent Freemasons have also been Luciferians, such as the Grand Commander of the Scottish Rite, Albert Pike, who is reputed to have said:

> We worship a god, but it is the god one adores without superstition... the Masonic religion should be by all of us initiates of the high degrees, maintained in the purity of the luciferian doctrine.

> If lucifer were not god, would Adonay (the God of the Christians) whose deeds prove cruelty, perfidy and hatred of man, barbarism and repulsion for

science, would Adonay and His priests, calumniate Him?

Yes, lucifer is god, and unfortunately Adonay is also God, for the eternal law is that there is no light without shade, no beauty without ugliness, no white without black, for the absolute can only exist as two gods. darkness being necessary for light to serve as its foil, as the pedestal is necessary to the statue, and the brake to the locomotive.

Thus, the doctrine of Satanism is heresy, and the true and pure philosophical religion is the belief in lucifer, the equal of Adonay, but lucifer, god of light and god of good, is struggling for humanity against Adonay, the god of darkness and evil.

Despite such statements, Albert Pike remains a revered figure in Illuminist circles. He is the only Confederate officer with an outdoor statue in Washington D.C.; it took a special act of Congress to bury him in the *House of the Temple*, a grand Roman-style mausoleum owned by the Supreme Council of the Scottish Rite of Freemasonry and located just blocks from the Capitol building.

All of this suggests to traditional monotheists that there are Luciferian/New Age cabals acting at the highest levels of Western civilization to transform the global religious and political order. Like the Enlightenment Illuminati, the Luciferians seek to establish world government, reduce the world population, disempower the Abrahamic religions, eliminate national and ethnic distinctions, and establish a new world system. Their ideology of Luciferian Illuminism is actually the basis of a new pantheistic (i.e. the cosmos is god), "green", eco-friendly global religion which will replace the old monotheistic faiths. A monotheist would say that the Luciferians worship the creation itself (the environment, the Earth, humanity, the cosmos) rather than the Creator, which is an inversion of the teachings of monotheism.

To many Muslims in particular, the rise of this inverted Luciferian, New Age ideology is associated with the impending arrival of the *Dajjal* – the Antichrist and Deceiver. It is grouped together with other modern innovations from the West, such as Freemasonry, Communism, Atheism, Zionism and Satanism, as evidence that the West is the cradle of a *Dajjal System* and a Satanic New World Order. As such, it is the mortal enemy of Islam, and must be fought until it is destroyed.

The Synarchists

Synarchism can be thought of as the hardline, "right wing" branch of Illuminism. It has been a guiding ideology behind the European Union project for almost a century, going back to the fascist movements of Mussolini and Hitler. It originated with a French occultist named Alexandre Saint-Yves in the 19th century and was championed by Pan-Europeanist Richard von Coudenhove-Kalergi and EU architect Alexandre_Kojève. Synarchism is essentially global corporatism, with privatized armies, aristocratic power structures and national governments subverted by international industrial and financial elites. Like other Illuminati factions, it has strong ties to Freemasonry – most notably the *Propaganda Due* (P2) Italian Lodge that attempted a Synarchist coup and controlled a private army as part of the notorious *Operation Gladio* (see below).

Synarchism has been strongly inspired by Nietzschean philosophy, according to which there is a small class of

"Übermenschen" ("Supermen") who are the rightful rulers of civilization. These Supermen are free to operate "beyond good and evil" – outside the normal moral values of the common people ("the herd"), as indeed they must to successfully rule. Synarchism has philosophical roots going back to Plato, who believed in a society ruled by an elite of "Philosopher-Kings", who propagated "noble lies" for the masses to enable civilization to function – the most useful noble lie being religion. Here again, we find that the hallmark of Illuminism is its hostility to religion and desire to curb its influence. What makes the Synarchists particularly clever is their willingness to cynically use religion and populist sentiments to manipulate the masses. Elite deception, manipulation and concealment of non-democratic power structures are hallmarks of Synarchist and Illuminist rule.

It should be noted that Synarchism, while it adopts many right wing forms such as fascism, militarism and corporatism, has just as much in common with Leninist or Stalinist Communism. Both ideologies are controlled by small, undemocratic elites. Both believe their societal models represent an "End of History" that should be adopted by all peoples of the world. Both seek to topple old allegiances to nation, race and religion and replace them with allegiances to a larger super-State project, such as the "Soviet Union", "European Union", "African Union" and "North American Union" – which are themselves just stepping stones to a global "New World Order".

Neoconservatism

In recent years, Synarchist ideology has been influential in America via "Neoconservatism" and the philosophy of of Leo Strauss. Straussians believe in an *esoteric* social order, in which the private beliefs of the elites are quite different from the ideology they profess to the rest of society. Among themselves, the elites are aristocratic and Nietzschean, believing themselves to be above the morality of the masses, who must be given different values in order to maintain the social order.

Neoconservatives are more idealistic than the Straussians, emphasizing the need to spread democracy around the world using military power, but they are every bit as deceptive. The "neocons" used blatant deception and manipulation to push for the invasion of Iraq, as part of an ambitious campaign to overthrow the "Axis of Evil", initiate a "New American Century" and install friendly governments throughout the world by force. Interestingly, these same neocons have allied themselves with jihadists for decades, seeing them as useful allies against non-New World Order regimes such as Russia, Syria and Iran. Indeed, in many cases – notably in Afghanistan in the 1980s – the neocons have directly armed and funded jihadist groups. Thus, we arrive at an interesting situation where the neoconservative branch of the Illuminati is actively creating its "antithesis", radical Islam, in order to offer a "synthesis" – the corporate, militarist Synarchist super-state.

Strategies of Tension

We see a pattern of supporting extremism wherever the Synarchists are influential. In the 1970s and 80s, Synarchist secret societies such as the Italian P2 backed the creation of an entire secret European army called *Gladio*, which was essentially an international terrorist organization used to destabilize non-Synarchist European governments. Gladio operatives were implicated in the bombing of a Bologna train station that killed 85 people, and a number of other terrorist attacks. Gladio's "strategy of tension" is a well-documented historical fact, which created an atmosphere of fear in Italy and led to security crackdown on the Leftist anti-Synarchists who were powerful at the time. Synarchists also sponsored "color revolutions" and fascist militias in Ukraine during its recent coup against the Russia-aligned government there. And now, with ISIS, we see some of the hallmarks of a Synarchist mercenary operation, including innovative tactics, slick propaganda and ruthless violence beyond anything we've seen from the Arab world in modern times.

All of these operations show clear signs of having a diabolical hidden hand behind them. They have killed thousands of people, created chaos and increased the potential for large scale wars, but may have an "ordo ab chao" (order out of chaos) strategy guiding them. By creating chaos, then offering a new order, the Synarchists are able to defeat resistance to their agenda. The entire "War on Terror", al Qaeda and indeed the 9/11 attacks themselves, may be driven by such a strategy. ISIS is also following an ordo ab chao strategy in Iraq and Syria – the "Management of Savery" model discussed earlier. All of this suggests that the Synarchists are the most dangerous and ruthless branch of the Illuminati operating in the world today, and are behind a vast conspiracy of terrorism, military expansion and global empire that is unmatched in its audacity and ambition.

The Zionists

One powerful group that is encountered repeatedly when trying to get to the root of both the Illuminati and their conflict with Islam are the *Zionists*. Zionists are those who support the existence of the state of Israel, centered in Jerusalem where the first two Jewish Temples once stood. Zionists aren't the same as Jews; there are many Christian

Zionists, and there are both conservative and "leftist" Jews who are anti-Zionist. In fact Zionism, the political ideology created by the architects of Israel such as Theodor Herzl and David Ben-Gurion, is quite different from traditional Judaism. Political Zionism incorporates ideas originating in Europe with the European Jews who founded modern Israel. These European Zionists subscribed to secular, socialist and Nietzschean ideologies, and were often hostile to both traditional Judaism and the original Semitic Jews who have lived in the Holy Land for millennia.

What is the connection between Zionism and the Illuminati? Historically, the main point of connection was the Freemasonic Lodges, which have been instrumental in fomenting revolutionary change in the Western world for the past few centuries. Freemasonry has long had a significant Jewish membership. Many of the early Masons in America were Jewish, including those who financed and fought in the Revolutionary War. Wherever Freemasonry has gained power, such as in the French Revolution, Jews are generally among the beneficiaries, as the religious authorities and monarchies who were hostile to them lose power. The state of Israel, like the U.S.A. and the French Republic, has had a strong Masonic influence from its inception. The Rothschilds banking family, who have been instrumental in financing Zionism from its inception, have been leading players in the Illuminati for centuries. Israel's first Prime Minister, Ben-Gurion, was a Mason, as have been most of its subsequent leaders; the Supreme Court building in Jerusalem, funded by the Rothschilds family, has a Masonic "All-Seeing Eye" at its entrance and an Illuminati pyramid on its roof.

Note also that the very name "Mason" refers to the stonemasons who built Solomon's Temple. The basic idea of Freemasonry is that each initiate is symbolically becoming a builder of the Temple of Solomon. The third degree Masonic initiation is an allegory of the biblical Hiram, architect of Solomon's Temple. By regaining control of Jerusalem and the Temple Mount and making possible the construction of a Third Temple, Israel is in a sense the culmination of the Masonic project. Yet non-traditional Eyptian, Babylonian and Kabbalist mysticism, language and symbolism pervades the Masonic doctrines. To many conservative Jews, Christians and Muslims alike, this Zionist-Masonic ideology is an imposter religion, and Israel is an imposter state.

The Illuminist or "New World Order" agenda of Israel is suggested by the statements of many leading Zionists; for example this one by Israel's founder and first prime minster, secularist David Ben-Gurion, from 1962:

> "With the exception of the U.S.S.R. as a federated Eurasian State, all other continents will become united in a world alliance at whose disposal will be an international police force. All armies will be abolished and there will be no more wars. In Jerusalem, the United Nations will build a shrine of the prophets to serve the federated union of all continents; this will be the seat of the Supreme Court of Mankind, to settle all controversies among the federated continents, as prophesied by Isaiah... "

Here Ben-Gurion is referring to the prophecy in the Book of Isaiah, in which the Temple is re-established at Mount Zion, war is abolished, and all the nations of the world make pilgrimages to Jerusalem to learn Torah law and submit to the Abrahamic God's judgement. Presumably, this entails submitting to Israeli religious or legal authority. This is the Zionist vision of the New World Order in a nutshell.

Zionism vs. Islam

The Illuminati-Islamist conflict becomes more understandable in light of the strong Zionist influence upon the Illuminati. Zionists, by bringing into existence the state of Israel in the heart of the Muslim world, are a mortal enemy of the Islamists. One of the basic tenets of Islam is that any land which has been conquered by Muslims must never be lost – indeed, it is compulsory upon Muslims to wage jihad to liberate any such territory and reclaim in for the Umma.

The situation is made even graver by the conflicting prophecies of the two sides. Muslims anticipate the arrival of *ad-Dajjal*, the Antichrist, who according to hadiths will attract a large following of Jews, and will be light-skinned with curly hair. Some scholars interpret this to mean that the Dajjal will be a Jew himself, who will establish a Satanic empire centered in Jerusalem. From the Islamic perspective, the founding of Israel in 1948, and the tremendous power the Zionists have acquired in the world since then, are strong signs that the Dajjal's civilization is being built and his arrival is near. Furthermore, since it is prophesied that a Muslim army will fight and defeat the Dajjal, Islamists see it as their divine role to fight the Zionists and their Dajjal System, ultimately destroying the "imposter" state of Israel and slaying the Dajjal.

THE NEW WORLD ORDER

The Illuminati's global project is often called the *New World Order*, or the *NWO* for short. The NWO plays a similar role for Illuminists as the Caliphate does for Islamists: it is their project of world transformation and domination, across every dimension of human existence – philosophical, political, cultural, economic and spiritual. Let us discuss the goals of this New World Order in more detail and describe some of its major conquests so far.

Ideological and Political Goals

Based on what we have already discussed, we can summarize the major ideological and political goals of the Illuminati groups as the following:

- The disempowerment and destruction of traditional religion. Separation of religion and state.

- The disempowerment and destruction of monarchies who don't adopt Enlightenment ideology.

- The disempowerment and destruction of any political system that opposes Enlightenment ideology.

- The breaking down of traditional bonds of tribe, race, nation and culture in favor of a globalized humanity, united by Enlightenment ideology.

- The creation of global institutions and a world government that adhere to Enlightenment ideology –

i.e. the "New World Order".

- Centralized control of the global economy via mega-corporations; control of global finance.

- The empowerment of an "Illuminated" elite who control the World Government and act as self-appointed rulers and myth-makers for the rest of humanity.

The Illuminati's tools to realize these goals include financial leverage, legal systems, political activism, non-governmental organizations, popular culture, news media, intellectual movements and technology. It is no exaggeration to say that Illuminati-aligned groups have a dominant position in all of these fields in the Western world today, and are aggressively propagating their ideology and control system to the rest of the planet. Quite simply, they are after *world domination.*

Wars and Revolutions

Above we listed one of the Illuminati's goals as "the disempowerment and destruction of any political system that opposes Enlightenment ideology." This goal has had particularly dramatic consequences for the world over the past two and a half centuries. For the old European and Russian Monarchies, the American Confederacy, Imperial Japan, Imperial China, Nazi Germany, the Soviet Union, and the Islamic Caliphate are just some of the powerful regimes the Illuminati has waged war upon and defeated. Indeed, we find that most of the major revolutions and wars in the Western world since the late 18th century have been *Illuminati Wars* – that is, they have been conflicts between various traditionalist or non-Enlightenment regimes and the insurgent Illuminati regimes based in America and Europe.

Thus it could truthfully be said that the Illuminati, being a revolutionary cult, has been by far the most disruptive and destructive force in world affairs since at least 1776. The currents they unleashed with their revolutions, first in the minds of the European intelligentsia, then on the streets and battlefields of America, France, Europe, and around the world, have brought war and chaos to a new level in modern times. While the non-Illuminist regimes they defeated may have been decadent, cruel or corrupt in many ways, their biggest failing was the fact that they *lost the war*, and now aren't here to tell their side of the story. The Illuminati, following an almost unbroken string of victories since 1776, has been able to remake the institutions and rewrite the history books to paint themselves as the heroes and saviors of mankind, and their enemies as the villains and damners.

Though they have vanquished many mighty foes and seized the highest thrones of world power, the Illuminati can never grow complacent, because the forces of human nature will always rebel against them and throw up fierce new challenges to their power. The latest, most menacing manifestation of this anti-Illuminati tendency is to be found in a reawakened and militant House of Islam. For the ideology of Islam stands in stark opposition to that of the Illuminati, and as Islam emerges from a period of quiet stagnation and colonization, it will mandate war against the heretical values of the Illuminist cults. European Christians, it should be remembered, fought a brutal Thirty Years War that brought Christendom to its knees and created an opening for a new order to emerge upon its ruins. The Muslim world has not been through such a process, and is full of historical grievances and a desire for revenge for the centuries of humiliation it has suffered at the hands of the infidel West. So the stage is set for the latest round of the Illuminati Wars, between the technocratic might of the Illuminati regimes and the pure religious passion of the holy warriors of Islam.

The United States of America

The Illuminati may have originated in Europe, but it achieved its its first great conquest with the establishment of the world's first Masonic republic: the United States of America. Freemasons played a key role in the founding of the United States. The Boston Tea Party that sparked the Revolution was instigated by members of the St. Andrews Masonic lodge of Boston. The first president of the USA, George Washington, was a Freemason. Benjamin Franklin was the president of the Philadelphia Lodge and a high-ranking Mason. Founding father and fifth president James Monroe was a Mason. About half of the generals in Washington's Continental Army were Masons, including Benedict Arnold.

There was resistance to Freemasonic and Illuminist influence in the United States from its earliest days. In 1796, John Quincy Adams warned: "I do conscientiously and sincerely believe that the Order of Freemasonry, if not the greatest, is one of the greatest moral and political evils under which the Union is now laboring." George Washington, acknowledged the existence of the Illuminati in a letter written in 1798:

> It was not my intention to doubt that, the Doctrines of the Illuminati, and principles of Jacobinism had not spread in the United States. On the contrary, no one is more truly satisfied of this fact than I am. The idea that I meant to convey, was, that I did not believe that the Lodges of Free Masons in this Country had, as Societies, endeavoured to propagate the

diabolical tenets of the first, or pernicious principles of the latter (if they are susceptible of seperation). That Individuals of them may have done it, or that the founder, or instrument employed to found, the Democratic Societies in the United States, may have had these objects; and actually had a seperation of the People from their Government in view, is too evident to be questioned.

Note how Washington acknowledges the Illuminati's probable role in the founding of the USA, but considers the Freemasons to be uncorrupted by their "diabolical tenets". This supports the claim made earlier that the Freemasons didn't become fully corrupted by Illuminati subversion until the 19th century.

Regardless of Washington's concerns, the first Freemasonic revolution was a fait accompli. Their revolution successful, the Illuminists incorporated Masonic symbols and rituals into the foundations of the U.S.A. and made it the model nation of the *Novus Ordo Seclorum* – the New World Order. The Great Seal of the United States, designed in 1782, established the Illuminist unfinished pyramid and Eye of Providence as national symbols (see the title page of this book). George Washington conducted a Masonic rite at the dedication of the new Capitol building in 1793, laying its cornerstone. The capitol city itself was designed by a Freemason and laid out in the shape of the ancient occult pentagram symbol. The Washington Monument, an obelisk in the ancient Egyptian design, was consecrated in a Masonic rite in 1848 with the laying of the cornerstone. The Statue of Liberty, famous symbol of American values, was given as a gift by the French Grand Orient Temple Masons to the Masons of America to celebrate the centennial of the world's first Masonic republic. The cornerstone of the Statue was laid in a Masonic ceremony; the torch in her hand symbolises "Enlightenment" and "Illumination."

The French Revolution

The French Revolution was the second great Freemasonic/Illuminist conquest after the American Revolution. It was a seminal event in the birth of the New World Order and the Illuminati's conquest of Western civilization.

One of the clearest signs of the Freemasonic nature of the French Revolution is found in *"Declaration of the Rights of Man and of the Citizen,"* a foundational document of Revolutionary France. The Declaration lays out the principles of the new French Republic, such as liberty, equality, democracy, secularism, universal human rights, sovereignty of the Nation, and freedom of speech. All of these principles are rooted in Enlightenment and Freemasonic philosophy, and were not part of the pre-Revolutionary European order. In fact, the Declaration was composed in the Masonic lodges of France, with input from Thomas Jefferson, author of the American Declaration of Independence and frequent visitor to Paris; Voltaire, member of the Parisian "Nine Sisters" Lodge; and Benjamin Franklin, ambassador to France from 1776 to 1785 and Grand Master of the Parisian Lodge from 1779 to 1781.

In addition to its Masonic principles and writers, the French Declaration contains explicit Masonic symbolism: the Eye of Providence, also seen on the Great Seal of the United States, is at the top of the document; below, the serpent eating its tail is the *Ouroboros*, an ancient symbol of alchemy and Hermeticism, which are central to Masonic occultism; the two pillars on each side are a common Freemasonic symbol

The "Declaration of the Rights of Man" original document

called *Boaz and Jachin,* which represent the two pillars at the entrance to King Solomon's Temple.

It is interesting to contrast the Articles of this Declaration with the principles of Sharia or other 'divine law'. For example:

Article III: *The principle of any sovereignty resides*

essentially in the Nation. No body, no individual can exert authority which does not emanate expressly from it.

Article VI: *The law is the expression of the general will. All the citizens have the right of contributing personally or through their representatives to its formation. ...*

These Articles are radical departures from the previous European regime, which granted final sovereignty and law-making ability to a monarch, and then to God. It also contradicts the fundamental principle of an Islamic state, which places final sovereignty with God alone, and gives no man the "divine right of Kings" nor the right to create laws which violate the Sharia. Thus, the French Revolution, by these Articles alone, is irreconcilable at its foundation with ISIS or any other Islamic state.

It is worth noting that *"The Universal Declaration of Human Rights"* adopted by the United Nations in 1948 (also in Paris) contains Masonic principles very similar to those of the French Declaration. In particular, Article 21.3 states:

> *The will of the people shall be the basis of the authority of government; this will shall be expressed in periodic and genuine elections which shall be by universal and equal suffrage and shall be held by secret vote or by equivalent free voting procedures.*

Here again, the idea that sovereignty belongs to the people rather than to God is made explicit, putting it in direct conflict with Islamic ideology. Article 28 is also interesting to note:

> *Everyone is entitled to a social and international order in which the rights and freedoms set forth in this*

Declaration can be fully realized.

Isn't saying that everyone is entitled to an "international order" that "fully realizes" these rights another way of saying that everyone on the planet must join the Masonic New World Order?

Note also that this U.N. Declaration was composed by a panel of mostly Westerners, with only a single man from the Muslim world, who was himself a Christian. Thus, the Islamic world had no input into this Declaration, nor in the founding of the United Nations. To Islamists, it is clear that the United Nations is non-Islamic at its foundation, and is essentially an Illuminati construct designed to impose its values and sociopolitical models upon the entire world.

THE DAJJAL SYSTEM

In this chapter, we consider the Illuminati and its "New World Order" project from a more Islamic perspective, to better understand how ISIS and similar groups view their main enemy.

A World Turned Upside Down

Muslims often refer to the civilization which the Illuminati has been setting up since the 18th century as the *Dajjal System*. This is the system of democracy, capitalism, liberalism, secularism and finance that has come to dominate the Western world since the American and French Revolutions. Under this system, things which are strictly *haram* (forbidden) under Islam (and which were previously forbidden by the Christian Church) have become halal (permitted), and things which are halal have become haram. Thus, the Illuminati's system has created an inverted, 'Satanic' civilization.

The Dajjal System can be said to have two gods: **money** and **pleasure.** We see these two gods celebrated in the Western media and entertainment industry constantly; "if it feels good do it" and "greed is good" seem to be their two guiding principles. Purchasing the latest smart phone, brand of beer, make of automobile, erectile dysfunction drug, etc. is touted in Western advertising as the height of human existence, while references to religion, God, etc. are all but non-existent. Thus, devout Muslims see a Western civilization which is celebrating the worldly desires of the animalistic lower self (nafs) and denigrating the higher, divine aspects of the self: Qalb (heart) and Ruh (spirit). They see the Dajjal System as a system which enslaves human beings to their material desires, compelling them to work endlessly to earn money, which they will then spend to satisfy their lusts. Furthermore, the New World Order is normalizing values such as homosexuality, abortion, feminism, alcohol and drug use, prostitution, usury, etc. which are strictly haram in Islam. To devout Muslims, these are all sure signs that the Illuminati's New World Order is a place designed by Shaytan (Satan), which is luring people to spend eternity in Jahannam (Hellfire).

This system is called the 'Dajjal System' by Muslims because they believe it is being set up in preparation for the arrival of Al-Masih ad-Dajjal – the False Messiah, Deceiver and Imposter prophesied in the hadiths. The Dajjal plays a similar role in Islam as the Antichrist in Christian theology – he will be a charismatic figure who appears near the end of time and attempts to deceive mankind that he is the Messiah. He will win a large following and will establish a Satanic empire that spreads corruption over the earth. At this point of mankind's greatest tribulations, Muhammad prophesied that Issa (Jesus) will return and slay the Dajjal and usher in the End of Time.

Muhammad also prophesied in the hadiths that there will be many signs of the Dajjal's arrival. Among the major signs, recorded by Ali, are the following:

- People will stop offering the prayers
- Dishonesty will be the way of life
- Falsehood will become a virtue
- People will mortgage their faith for worldly gain

- Usury and bribery will become legitimate
- There will be acute famine at the time
- There will be no shame amongst people
- Many people would worship Satan
- There would be no respect for elderly people

To devout Muslims, most of these signs have already come to pass in the Illuminati's Western civilization. The unprecedented levels of materialism, secularism, greed, usury, libertine behavior, deception and open Satanism on display in the West today seem to be confirming their worst fears. And the fact that this inverted civilization has become so powerful, spreading its 'Dajjalic' values across the world and into Muslim lands via its mass media, is strong evidence that it is indeed the civilization which heralds the coming of the Dajjal, and which therefore must be fought to the End. As Muhammad is recorded as saying in one hadith:

> "The end of time will not come until someone will tell a lie and it will immediately reach the horizons of the Earth."

The ability to instantly propagate a lie to the whole world has never been available before now, with the advent of global telecommunications and the internet. Is the end of time at hand?

The One-Eyed Civilization

The eye symbol used on the Great Seal of the USA is known as the "Eye of Providence"; the eye with rays emanating from it are said to represent the eye of God watching over mankind, and radiating his goodness onto them. The eye is located in the triangular capstone of a pyramid, which represents the Messiah in Jewish theology.

Above the pyramid are the Latin words "Annuit Cœptis", which means "He favors our enterprise." This symbolism has been used by the Freemasons since the late 18th century, though they claim it wasn't adopted until after the founding of the USA.

This symbolism is highly significant to Muslims, because one of the prophesied characteristics of the Dajjal that Muhammad spoke of is that he will be *one-eyed* – he will have one eye which is blind and deformed like a "bulging grape". He will also be the "false Messiah", who will deceive many Jews that he is their savior. This alignment of symbolism with prophecy has convinced many Muslims that America is the seed of the Dajjal's civilization. The eye on the Great Seal of the United States, the prevalence of one-eye symbolism in Hollywood, the music industry, corporations, the dollar bill, and other powerful propagators of the Illuminati's New World Order, all suggest that there is a diabolical agenda at work. If this symbolism isn't a foreshadowing of the coming Dajjal, what is its purpose? And if it *is* Antichrist symbolism, is it being used deliberately by a Satanic elite, or are they unwitting pawns in an unearthly game, played by powers and principalities beyond the mundane world?

Zionism

Zionism is seen by many Muslims as a key element of the Dajjal System. The rise of a powerful Jewish state in the heart of the Muslim world, with technological, financial and propaganda resources that stretch across the globe, is seen as a harbinger of the appearance of the false Messiah, the Dajjal.

What is the connection between Zionism, Judaism and the Dajjal? In the hadiths, it is said that the Dajjal will be a one-eyed, curly-haired, stocky young Jewish man. He will recruit an army of 70,000 Jews, who will attempt to conquer Mecca and Medina. He will seduce people across the world by offering hell disguised as heaven, and heaven disguised as hell. According to some scholars, his power center will Jerusalem, from which he will build a global empire. To Muslims these prophecies are consistent with current events, in that Israel has powerful connections to the Zionist centers of global influence in Hollywood, Wall Street, Madison Avenue, Washington D.C. And Silicon Valley, and may be angling to become the center of this entire web of global control. Furthermore, the values propagated by the Zionist media are the inverse of traditional Islamic ones, portraying "hell as heaven", and vice versa.

To Muslims, Zionism is consistent with the "imposter" Dajjal System in that it is an "imposter" ideology masquerading as Judaism. Zionism, as formulated by Theodor Herzl in the late 19th century and pursued by leading Zionists such as David Ben-Gurion, founder of Israel, has incorporated many non-Judaic elements into its ideology. The original European Zionists were often critical of traditional Judaism, and took their inspiration from such modern secular European thinkers such as Karl Marx and Friedrich Nietzsche. Israel remains to this day dominated by European "Ashkenazi" Jews who are culturally quite different from the native "Shephardhi" Jews that Arabs lived with peacefully for centuries. Thus, to many Muslims, the appearance of the culturally alien and aggressive European Zionists into the region in recent times looks like some kind of diabolical disruption, and another sign that the age of the Dajjal is at hand.

ILLUMINATI STRATEGY

Previously, we discussed some of the strategies that ISIS and other Islamists are using to try to defeat the Illuminati and impose their Islamic world order. What is the Illuminati's strategy? How have they achieved so much already, and how will they advance their New World Order agenda further? Below are ten key tactics and principles that the Illuminati have used for centuries to gain power:

Ten Tactics

Divide and Conquer

Divide and conquer is an age-old tactic of rulers: simply divide a group you wish to conquer into warring camps, so they are too weakened from fighting each other to resist your advances. The Illuminists of the British Empire were masters of this tactic, playing various tribal groups against each other in the lands they colonized. Elites in NWO "democracies" do this by dividing the electorate into parties, all of which are controlled, so they will fight each other rather than the puppet-masters who are pulling the strings. Some even suggest that Islamic terrorist groups are being used to stir up sectarian conflicts in the Middle East as part of an Illuminati divide and conquer plan to prevent Muslims from uniting against them.

Ordo ab Chao

Ordo ab chao is a Freemasonic expression that refers to the strategy of creating chaos intentionally to disrupt an existing order so it can be replaced by a new one. The French Revolution was perhaps the Illuminati's greatest ordo ab chao operation – plunging France into chaos to destroy the *Ancien Régime,* then ushering in a new order of democracy and secularism that would spread across Europe. The "strategy of tension" discussed earlier was another such project. More recently, the invasion of Iraq by the United States that plunged the region into chaos was a grand ordo ab chao operation, but it's not clear what new order is going to replace the ongoing chaos (Greater Israel? The Persian Empire? The Islamic State?) Note that another name for ordo ab chao tactics is *terrorism.*

Ends Justify the Means

The Illuminati follow the Machiavellian principle that any action can be justified if it serves the right goal. Adam Weishaupt himself is quoted as saying: "Behold our secret. Remember that the end justifies the means." Thus, terrorism, revolution, deception, murder, subversion, etc. are all acceptable, as long that they are furthering Illuminati objectives such as the New World Order. This principle explains ruthless operations such as the French Revolution and the Strategy of Tension, which resulted in thousands of deaths and widespread suffering. It contrasts with most religions, which contain ethical laws that aren't to be violated no matter what the objective. For example, in Islam, many actions are *haram* (forbidden) in all circumstances: one cannot drink even if it cures certain ailments, or kill innocents even to establish Sharia. The Islamist ideologue Sayyid Qutb clearly stated:

> He is not a Muslim who claims that the ends justify the means. Such a principle is alien to Islamic thinking and cannot fit with Islamic sensitivities. Within the human self there can be no gulf to separate the ends from the means.

Even ISIS uses the Quran and Sunnah to justify its most heinous actions, and doesn't believe it is using haram means even when it beheads, enslaves and crucifies its enemies. For the Illuminati, there are no inherent limits on its actions.

False Dialectics

The *false dialectic* is the tactic of offering a limited menu of choices which all serve the dominant Illuminist agenda. It is a false choice, intended to control discourse so that one doesn't ask about items not on the menu – while simultaneously creating an illusion of freedom. A prime example is the two party electoral system in the USA, where one is offered the choice of voting for a Republican or a Democrat, both of whom are part of the same system and have been hand-picked by elites for their willingness to go along with the program. This two party dialectic has the effect of excluding all other parties and perspectives; the Republicans exclude the far Right, the Democrats exclude the far Left, and both will collude to exclude anyone who seriously threatens the system itself. This methodology is widely used, not just in elections, but in media debates, economic policies, religious discourse, etc.

Problem-Reaction-Solution

Problem-reaction-solution, also known as a *Hegelian dialectic*, is a process whereby, when Illuminists wants to implement some new policy, they manufacture a problem, which creates a reaction, which generates the solution they were looking for. For example, if the Illuminati wants to change the regimes of some Muslim countries, they could engineer a spectacular false-flag terrorist attack against America that frames Muslims. This creates a reaction of outrage and a desire for revenge against the Muslim world. This anger is then vented in the invasion of the targeted regimes. Sound familiar?

Rule by Deception

The Illuminati operates by deception; they conceal their true agenda, and indeed their very existence. Like Leo Strauss, they believe the elite must wear masks, because their true beliefs would be destructive to society if they were adopted by the masses. Deception is necessary because people can't handle the truth about Illuminism, and they would reject it and revolt if it were revealed.

Control of Culture

One of the linchpins of the Illuminati system is control of culture. By owning the news media, television networks movie studios, music, publishing and advertising industries, etc., the Illuminists can ensure that the messages they favor are part of mainstream culture, and hostile messages are marginalized. The Illuminati have been very successful in expanding the reach of their cultural system across much of the world, using Hollywood, Madison Avenue, CNN, etc. to establish global brands and cultural norms. This expansion has brought them into conflict with other cultural systems and created great resentment at the way it has disrupted other traditions – notably in the Islamic world.

Control of Money

The Illuminati banker Mayer Amschel Rothschild famously said: "permit me to issue and control the money of a nation, and I care not who makes its laws!" Financial control is perhaps the most powerful of all the Illuminati's weapons; it allows them to purchase politicians, blackmail entire countries, sabotage enemy regimes, buy up opinion-making apparatus (media, think tanks, etc.), fund mercenary armies, and enslave the world with debt. A key Illuminati financial coup was the Federal Reserve Act of 1913, which essentially gave control of the U.S. money supply to a cabal of private international bankers – and hence gave them a hidden, controlling hand over the entire government. The abandonment of the dollar gold standard was another major coup; it means that dollars are no longer a stable store of wealth, being at the mercy of central bankers who can destroy its value at any moment by financial manipulation. Thus, those whose wealth is held in dollars are effectively slaves to the central bankers – who are themselves controlled by the Illuminati.

Control of Narratives

Another tactic that Illuminists use very effectively is *narrative control*. The idea is to lay claim to the future; to assert that one's own goals are the inevitable destiny toward which the world is evolving, and that everyone opposed to them are blacksliders, holdouts and reactionaries, swimming against the tide of history. This is a type of Hegelian dialectic; at its root is the idea that there is one best model for society, which all reasonable people should agree on, and all other options are incorrect or evil. Illuminists have been very successful at controlling narratives in this way due to their tremendous influence over the media, entertainment industry and intellectual discourse. The danger of this kind of "progressive" thinking is that it creates a pretext for global tyranny.

Indigenous Puppets

Another tactic the Illuminati employs masterfully is the use of controlled indigenous representatives from the various societies they wish to influence. The Illuminist, imperialist British were masters of this method; they would co-opt elites from the nations they sought to conquer, bring them into their elite power circles, then present them in the Illuminist media as the enlightened representatives of their people. The entire British empire was built upon the co-option of coastal elites, who became their proxy rulers over indigenous populations around the world. This is the root of the hostility of the Muslim masses to the Westernized puppet leaders who still rule over them today. In the West itself, Illuminists employ this tactic frequently, bringing representatives of various demographic groups into their ranks and promoting them in their opinion-making apparatus (Barack Obama, darling of many high level Illuminists, is a good example of this). The formless, rootless nature of the Illuminists, who have no strong allegiance to any particular tribe or nationality, allows them to co-opt people from every background and use them as puppets in a very Machiavellian and ingenious game of global control.

War & Subversion

Three World Wars?

According to a story well known in "Illuminati-watcher" circles, a letter written in 1871 describes three world wars that would need to be fought to bring about the Illuminati's New

World Order. The letter was allegedly written by Albert Pike, the leading American Freemason of his time, to Giuseppe Mazzini, Italian Freemason, revolutionary and reputed Illuminati leader. According to witnesses, this letter was on display in the British Museum Library until 1977, when it was removed.

The letter predicts a first world war would be fought to overthrow the Russian czars and establish Communism as an anti-Christian world power. The second world war would enable the formation of the Zionist state of Israel and further empower Communism. The letter concludes with the following prediction of World War III:

Third World War: Zionism vs. Islam

The Third World War must be fomented by taking advantage of the differences caused by the "agentur" of the "Illuminati" between the political Zionists and the leaders of Islamic World. The war must be conducted in such a way that Islam (the Moslem Arabic World) and political Zionism (the State of Israel) mutually destroy each other.

Meanwhile the other nations, once more divided on this issue will be constrained to fight to the point of complete physical, moral, spiritual and economical exhaustion... We shall unleash the Nihilists and the atheists, and we shall provoke a formidable social cataclysm which in all its horror will show clearly to the nations the effect of absolute atheism, origin of savagery and of the most bloody turmoil.

Then everywhere, the citizens, obliged to defend themselves against the world minority of revolutionaries, will exterminate those destroyers of civilization, and the multitude, disillusioned with christianity, whose deistic spirits will from that moment be without compass or direction, anxious for an ideal, but without knowing where to render its adoration, will receive the true light through the universal manifestation of the pure doctrine of Lucifer, brought finally out in the public view.

This manifestation will result from the general reactionary movement which will follow the destruction of Christianity and atheism, both conquered and exterminated at the same time.

So according to this letter, the final stage of the Luciferian Illuminati's grand plan is to discredit Christianity, Islam, Zionism and atheism simultaneously by provoking an apocalyptic war between Israel and the Muslim world that drags in the Christian West and the Communist East. In the aftermath of this vast devastation, people will be starving for something new, and the Illuminati will move to fill the void by openly promoting their Luciferian religion.

We should point out here that the evidence for the existence of this letter is flimsy, and there is a good chance that it was fabricated. Nevertheless, the letter has become so notorious that it has influenced not just Western conspiracy theorists, but many Muslims. Numerous books and videos are available in the Muslim world that discuss this letter and its conspiracy to wage war against Islam as if it were a settled fact. It is worth considering as "black propaganda" that is influencing Muslims to militantly resist the New World Order, even if the letter itself is untrue.

Ideological Subversion

Another tactic which the Illuminists are very adept at is ideological subversion: weakening, altering or discrediting an opposing ideology by infiltrating its ranks and propagating a watered-down or counterfeit version of the ideology which will be less threatening. A prime example of this was the Illuminist attempt to create so-called "Rand Muslims" in the first years of the "War on Terror".

In 2003, the Rand Corporation, an important Illuminist security think tank, released a paper called *"Civil Democratic Islam: Partners, Resources, and Strategies."* The paper describes strategies to promote moderate Islam and marginalize fundamentalism. Under the heading "Assertively Promote the Values of Western Democratic Modernity", the author proposes to "create and propagate a model for prosperous, moderate Islam by identifying and actively aiding countries or regions or groups with the appropriate views. Publicize their successes." The paper calls for inserting the message of "democratic Islam" into school curricula, publishing and distributing moderate Islamic scholars at subsidized cost, encouraging Sufism (mystical, non-political Islam), promoting awareness of pre-Islamic traditions, giving modernist Muslims a media platform and making them a "hip" counterculture to attract youth, publicizing the evils of fundamentalism, and encouraging divisions between different types of Muslims.

These are all classic Illuminist social engineering techniques which have been employed to transform cultures so they will accept the NWO system. Having used such techniques to break down and conquer the formerly Christian West, the Machiavellian Illuminists have now set their sights on doing the same thing in the Muslim world. The effect of the Rand proposal would be to create a more docile, Westernized "Rand Muslim", whose main enemy is not their NWO puppet leaders, but the Islamists in their midst. Not surprisingly, many Islamists have condemned the Rand scheme and warned Muslims against it.

AN IDEOLOGICAL COMPARISON

A War of Worldviews

Now that we have described the basic ideologies of ISIS and the Illuminati, let us compare them directly to get a clearer picture of the black-and-white, Manichean nature of this conflict. The table below summarizes the two ideologies:

	ISIS	Illuminati
Regime	Global Caliphate	New World Order
Government Structure	Islamic Theocracy	Secular/Luciferian Synarchy
Governing Law	Exoteric; Sharia law for all	Esoteric; one law for elites, one for masses
Philosophy	Monotheism; Quran is absolute truth	Nietzschean; Man determines truth
Attitude to Life & Death	Fears Hellfire, loves death & martyrdom	Fears death and suffering, loves life
Revolutionary Events	Muhammad's revelations & jihads	The Enlightenment/ French Revolution
Ideal World	7th century Arabia	The Federation/Matrix

	ISIS	Illuminati
Goal of Life	Submit to God	Become like a god
Financial System	Gold-backed currency, no usury	Fiat currency, usury-based
Culture	Austere, spartan, devout	Bohemian, liberal, sacrilegious

From this table, we see that in many ways, the two projects are polar opposites. The Islamic system derives from a belief in a supra-rational, divinely-inspired source of truth: Allah, Lord of the Worlds, who revealed his laws through his Prophets and the Quran. Allah's laws are eternal, unchanging and unchallengeable by man. The Illuminist system, by contrast, is based on the belief that "man is the measure of all things"; that by his reason and free will alone man can determine what is moral, good and lawful. Islamism is monotheistic and absolutist; Illuminism is atheistic and existentialist.

Islamism and Illuminism also have inverse ideas about human history and destiny. Islamists believe in an ideal past – a golden age of the perfect man, the Prophet, and his heroic companions, the Sahaba, after which each generation was less pious. Islamists consider this world just a temporary test – a place of material illusions and "devil's traps" that the believer must navigate on his way to an eternal fate in paradise or hellfire. Illuminism focuses on this world and imagines a better future toward which society is progressing, leaving behind the a dark and ignorant past. Illuminists also subscribe to the Kabbalistic/Hermetic notion that human beings are evolving toward godhood through reason, science and technology, with no limits to our potential. But what the Illuminized Western world has called "progress", "liberation" and "enlightenment" over the past few centuries, the Islamists see as a process of sinking deeper into godlessness, materialism and glorification of base desires.

Thus it is clear that the two projects are diametrically opposed at their philosophical foundations. The Islamic vision of society is similar to the medieval Christian one, before the coming of the Enlightenment and the Illuminati revolutions that radically transformed the West. In effect, the Illuminati's modern struggle with Islam is a replay of its struggle with Christianity; just as the Illuminists managed to conquer Christendom by converting elite intellectuals and using them as a vanguard against the priesthood, today we see the Illuminists converting elites in the Muslim world and pitting them against the imams and traditionalist masses in their media. To Illuminists, it is an article of faith that Muslims will eventually embrace the secular values and "progress" of the West, just as Christians did centuries ago. But this matter has not yet been decided, and there doesn't appear to be much chance of a peaceful resolution. Since the Illuminists don't originate from within Islamic civilization, it is much more difficult for them to conquer Islam from within as they did with Christian civilization. They may have to resolve their differences on the battlefield.

Islamism and Illuminism: Two Sides of One Coin?

Islamists and Illuminists have radically different goals, but in some important ways they are very similar. One might say they are two sides of the same coin; the yin and the yang, the thesis and antithesis of a larger dialectic. What does this mean? For one, both ideologies are *Universalist:* they offer a philosophy and a model of society which they claim is best for all mankind, not just for one race, tribe or nation. Sayyid Qutb made Islamism's Universalism clear when he said:

> This religion is not merely a declaration of the freedom of the Arabs, nor is its message confined to the Arabs. It addresses itself to the whole of mankind, and its sphere of work is the whole earth. God is the Sustainer not merely of the Arabs, nor is His providence limited to those who believe in the faith of Islam. God is the Sustainer of the whole world. This religion wants to bring back the whole world to its Sustainer and free it from servitude to anyone other than God. In the sight of Islam, the real servitude is following laws devised by someone, and this is that servitude which in Islam is reserved for God alone.

Both also see themselves as "liberation" and "revolutionary" ideologies, which come to free all peoples from the bonds of oppressive traditional systems such as nationalism, monarchy and tribalism. Qutb called such systems *Jahil*, meaning they are from an age of ignorance, before Muhammad's revolution brought the final divine guidance to mankind. Islamist revolutionaries consider all non-Islamic systems to be systems of enslavement of men by other men, in the form of democracy, plutocracy, monarchy, dictatorship, etc. All such systems prevent Islam from being practiced in its totality; hence Islamists strive to annihilate such systems and "free" mankind to choose to practice Islam. As Qutb put it:

> Because this religion proclaims the freedom of man on the earth from all authority except that of God, it is confronted in every period of human history- yesterday, today, or tomorrow - with obstacles of

beliefs and concepts, physical power, and the obstacles of political, social, economic, racial and class structures. ...

If the actual life of human beings is found to be different from this declaration of freedom, then it becomes incumbent upon Islam to enter the field with preaching as well as the movement, and to strike hard at all those political powers which force people to bow before them and which rule over them, unmindful of the commandments of God, and which prevent people from listening to the preaching and accepting the belief if they wish to do so. After annihilating the tyrannical force, whether it be in a political or a racial form, or in the form of class distinctions within the same race, Islam establishes a new social, economic and political system, in which the concept of the freedom of man is applied in practice. ...

Indeed, Islam has the right to take the initiative. Islam is not a heritage of any particular race or country; this is God's religion and it is for the whole world. It has the right to destroy all obstacles in the form of institutions and traditions which limit man's freedom of choice. It does not attack individuals nor does it force them to accept its beliefs; it attacks institutions and traditions to release human beings from their poisonous influences, which distort human nature and which curtail human freedom.

In the case of the Illuminati, their revolution divides history between the "Jahiliyya" of the pre-Enlightenment world and the "Illumination" of the post-Enlightenment, post-

American and French Revolutionary world. Illuminists spread their "Shariah" of "democracy", "freedom" and "progress" via their global media, propagandizing directly to the populations of target nations and routing around the local cultural control systems. The obstacles to the New World Order system that must be removed are the non-Illuminist cultural, legal and religious authorities that still rule in many parts of the world – especially Islam. These obstacles are removed by "preaching" – i.e. introducing the television, movies, music, and internet propaganda from the NWO centers; and by "physical jihad" – i.e. drone strikes, military invasions, coups, revolutions and economic warfare against regimes that successfully resist the NWO's efforts to conquer by propaganda.

Thus, we see that the Islamists and the Illuminists are playing similar games, with different methods but the same totalist goals: the removal of obstacles to their imperialism, the defeat of rival ideologies, the use of force to impose their societal models, and the establishment of a world-dominating global empire.

Weaknesses of the New World Order

On paper, the war between ISIS and the Illuminati would seem to be no contest. The Illuminati dominates the global media and cultural apparatus, has crushing military and economic superiority and controls the global financial system. How can a band of fanatics, armed only with faith in a 7th century Arab prophet, an archaic cultural model, meager resources and light weapons, hope to compete with the Illuminati's global empire? Surely the Islamists will be crushed, being outmoded barbarians with nothing to offer mankind in the 21st century?

In fact, despite all its power, the Illuminati's New World Order suffers from some potentially fatal flaws which the Islamists are exploiting. Here are a few of the major weak points of the New World Order ideology, from the author's point of view:

Loss of Religion

From its inception, the Illuminati has targeted organized religion and sought to curb its power. Their campaign has been very successful, but it has also made it the enemy of a great many people, who find in religion a vital source of values, meaning and community. And as the Illuminati has expanded its influence outside the West, it has come into conflict with societies where religion is still a powerful force, having not been marginalized by centuries of Illuminist and Enlightenment revolution. This is particularly true in the Muslim world, where Islam remains integral to the fabric of society. As the anti-religious nature of the New World Order becomes more apparent, we are beginning to see an alliance emerge between Muslims and Christians against the secular/'Satanic' NWO. The point is, the Illuminati has not yet succeeded in replacing traditional religion, and remains vulnerable to religious revivals and radicalism – not just in the Muslim world, but in its strongholds in the West.

Lack of Traditions or Identity

By its nature, the New World Order disconnects human beings from the traditions and sources of identity that have defined them for centuries. By promoting a radical vision of a unified world, without divisions of nation, religion, tribe or culture, the NWO is undermining billions of people's greatest sources of strength. Will humanity become a globalized, deracinated species, who abandon their own 'outmoded' traditions and come to view them with scorn? This seems to be the Illuminati's program, but it is provoking strong reactions by tribes with other ideas. Chief among these tribes is the the Umma of fundamentalist Islam, who can see that the NWO has little place for them in their world order, and are leaving them little choice but to submit or fight. There is also a significant counter-movement of nationalists and traditionalists within the West, who are threatening to undo much of what the NWO globalists have achieved.

No Myth Worth Fighting For

A related problem with NWO ideology is its lack of an inspiring myth or cause worth fighting for. Bin Laden called Western soldiers 'paper tigers' and said: "Your problem will be how to convince your troops to fight, while our problem will be how to restrain our youths to wait for their turn in fighting and in operations." What will inspire the citizens of the NWO to fight going forward? Will young men really risk their lives defending societies ruled by grey technocrats, financiers and corporate puppets? We are already seeing young men raised in the comfort of the West defecting to the jihadists; clearly they find something about that way of life attractive. It seems that the materialistic, hedonistic lifestyles encouraged in the NWO failed to inspire them, and the life of pleasure-seeking and corporate servitude couldn't compare to the glories of jihad. As the NWO machine continues to transform the world into a techno-corporate "prison planet" or a gilded cage, we can expect many more people from within the belly of the beast to seek radical alternatives – and what could be more radical that joining the jihad to destroy the NWO beast itself?

George Orwell understood this problem back in 1940, when the NWO faced a similar threat in the form of Fascism:

[Hitler] has grasped the falsity of the hedonistic attitude to life. Nearly all western thought since the last war, certainly all "progressive" thought, has assumed tacitly that human beings desire nothing beyond ease, security and avoidance of pain. In such a view of life there is no room, for instance, for patriotism and the military virtues. ... Hitler ... knows that human beings don't only want comfort, safety, short working-hours, hygiene, birth-control and, in general, common sense; they also, at least intermittently, want struggle and self-sacrifice, not to mention drums, flags and loyalty-parades. However they may be as economic theories, Fascism and Nazism are psychologically far sounder than any hedonistic conception of life. ... Whereas Socialism, and even capitalism in a more grudging way, have said to people "I offer you a good time," Hitler has said to them "I offer you struggle, danger and death," and as a result a whole nation flings itself at his feet.

Orwell's words about Hitler and the appeal of Nazism apply just as well today to ISIS and the appeal of jihadism. Will the world have to fight another great war to quench its thirst for struggle, danger and death? It seems quite likely.

Weaknesses of Islamism

I will not spend much time describing the weaknesses of Islamism here. This is not because I am in the Islamist camp, but simply because if you are reading this, you have probably already absorbed many anti-Islamist criticisms via your culture, media and educational system. Briefly, some of the major weaknesses of Islamism are:

- Inability to prove its claims about Allah, Muhammad and the Quran.
- Inflexibility; unwillingness to change to meet the needs of a changing world.
- Hostility to innovation makes Islamist society stagnant and economically and technologically inferior to West.
- The harshness of Sharia law repels modern people.
- Preference for afterlife over the *dunya* – the things of this world – makes it a loser in this world.
- Women are oppressed by Western standards, and aren't allowed to achieve their full potential.

THE WAR SO FAR

Let us now discuss the Islamist-Illuminati conflict in more detail, including the major events up to now, their symbolic significance, and where the conflict may be going in the future.

September 11th in New York

September 11th, 2001 was the day the war between Islamists and the Illuminati exploded into the world's awareness. The symbolism could not be clearer: two airplanes piloted by jihadist *kamikazes* were flown into the "twin towers" in New York – mighty symbols of the New World Order's financial power – reducing them both to rubble. The twin towers are a grandiose expression of the *Boaz and Jachin* Masonic two pillar symbolism, and the Islamists may have targeted them as part their symbolic war upon the Freemasonic/Illuminist New World Order. In any case, it's clear that on that day an age of apocalyptic Islamic jihad began, and the Illuminati was put on notice that a ruthless and ingenious old enemy had re-awakened.

Friday the 13th in Paris

If there is one day that could be said to mark the onset of an era of world war between ISIS and the New World

Order, it was Friday, the 13th of November, 2015. The attacks by eight ISIS terrorists on that day in Paris escalated the war between ISIS and the Illuminati to a terrifying new level. By calmly slaughtering over one hundred young people in a music hall, coordinated with suicide bombings and shootings elsewhere, eight terrorists forced the entire nation of France into a state of lockdown and fear not seen since World War II. For France and Europe, the events of that day traumatized them much like the attacks of September 11th, 2001 did to Americans, and marked the onset of an escalating war against global jihadism.

A Symbolic Message?

Beyond the obvious declaration of war, the attacks of Friday, November 13, 2015 have an esoteric dimension which is surely significant in the larger war we are discussing here. For on Friday the 13th in Paris 708 years earlier, the King of France and the Catholic Church cracked down on the Knights Templar, raiding their Paris headquarters and arresting, torturing and killing many of the organization's leaders. This crackdown would be the beginning of the end for the Templars as an overt organization, but many believe that their influence lived on in secret, resurfacing centuries later as the Freemasons, the Illuminati and other groups who would get their revenge upon the Church and monarchies of Europe and totally remake the world.

The point here is that there is an occult dimension to this war that usually goes right over the heads of observers – particularly of Westerners who have so little awareness of history and religious symbolism. Islamists have shown repeatedly that they place great importance on important dates, locations, and other symbolic elements of their attacks. They use the symbolic dimension of warfare as a kind of "force multiplier" and "black magical" technique, to not only terrorize the population at large, but to demoralize the Illuminati elites who do understand the symbolism. By attacking Paris on that particular day, the Islamists seem to be sending the Illuminist and Freemasonic heirs of the Knights Templar a symbolic message: we are striking another crushing blow against you on this day, at the birthplace of your Illuminati project, and we will defeat you just as you were defeated before.

A 20 Year Plan for World Domination

Where is the Islamist-Illuminati war going in the future? On the Islamist side, it is instructive to look at an al Qaeda '20 year plan' released to the Western media in 2005. The plan, written by a former Egyptian Colonel and high-ranking al Qaeda member named Saif al-Adel, outlines the group's strategy to defeat the West and establish a global Islamic Caliphate by 2020. It was allegedly conceived in 1996; if true, it shows an almost prophetic ability to predict (and create) the future. The plan is divided into the following seven stages, beginning in the year 2000:

2000-2003: The Awakening

Plan: Strike a powerful blow against the "head of the snake", the United States, provoking an attack on the Muslim world, thus awakening the Muslim masses.
Results: The 9/11 attacks and the invasions of Afghanistan and Iraq achieved this stage.

2003-2006: Opening Eyes

Plan: Make the world aware of the Islamic community. Recruit young men and turn the organization into a wider movement. Make Iraq the center of global jihad operations.

Results: With the U.S. Invasion of Iraq and the influx of jihadis there, including the founding of *al Qaeda in Iraq* (father of ISIS), this stage was largely achieved.

2007-2010: Arising and Standing Up

Plan: This stage calls for focusing on Syria, as well as attacks on Turkey and Israel.

Results: This stage was a bit off; the Syrian uprising didn't begin until 2011.

2010-2013: Recovery

Plan: During this stage, the hated secular Arab governments will be overthrown. Attacks against oil suppliers and cyber-attacks against the U.S. will be carried out.

Results: This stage was highly prophetic, considering that many Arab governments were toppled during the "Arab Spring" and Islamists gained power in Egypt and threatened to take over Libya, Syria and Iraq.

2013-2016: Islamic Caliphate

Plan: An Islamic state or Caliphate will be established during this period. Western influence in the Islamic world will be dramatically weakened, allowing the Islamic state to initiate a new world order.

Results: Another direct hit. The establishment of the Islamic State's Caliphate in Iraq and Syria in 2014 was right on target, ushering in a new era of jihadist aggression and global anxiety.

2016-2020: Total Confrontation

Plan: With the establishment of the Caliphate, an Islamic army will launch offensive wars to unite the Muslims, purge Muslim lands of apostates, defeat infidel states and expand the borders of Islam.

Results: The attack in Paris on November 13, 2015 and other ISIS-inspired attacks appear to be initiating this stage on schedule.

2020 Onward: Definitive Victory

Plan: The forces of the Caliphate will be victorious. The world will be so beaten down by one and a half billion Muslims that it will admit defeat.

Results: To be determined...

The plan described above has been remarkably accurate, if not prophetic. Things that sounded totally outlandish in 1996 when the plan was formulated, such as provoking the U.S. Into major wars, the overthrow of Arab governments and the establishment of a Caliphate, have occurred as predicted.

Note that the period of 2016 to 2020 is projected to be a period of "total confrontation" between Islamists and the West. And as if to herald this most dangerous new phase, the end of 2015 brought the horrific attacks in Paris that saw 130 Parisians get slaughtered in their own streets, and 2016 brought the Brussels airport bombing that killed 32. At the same time, hundreds of thousands of refugees from Middle Eastern war-zones began flooding into Europe, with indications that there are many ISIS sympathizers among them. Surely ISIS is infiltrating many trained fighters among the refugees as well. Indeed, the mastermind of the Paris attacks himself, Abdelhamid Abaaoud, may have returned to Europe from Syria with the flood of refugees. So it begins to look as though an Islamist invasion of Europe is underway.

And if eight people could put France into a state of total lock-down and panic, imagine what hundreds or even thousands could do! We may be looking at the onset of a total war-zone in Europe in the next few years. Again, the Islamist 20 year plan is looking remarkably prophetic.

A Propaganda War

So far, the Islamist-Illuminati war has been as much a propaganda war as a physical war. The Islamist strategist Abu Bakr Naji wrote of the need to break the "halo of invincibility" that hovers around the modern West; what he is really talking about is breaking the Illuminati's vast system of global cultural control and propaganda, which celebrates those who comport with its agenda, vilifies those who resist, and paints its New World Order project as the invincible, inevitable destiny of mankind. Some of the main tools of this Illuminist "halo-generating" propaganda machine are Hollywood, the news media (CNN, BBC, etc.) and the music, advertising and publishing industries. By dominating the global news, entertainment and myth-making apparatus, the Illuminati can mold minds on a global scale, marginalize opposing worldviews such as Islam, and propagate replacements for traditional religion such as "sex, drugs and rock & roll" hedonism, materialism, and secular humanism.

The Illuminati is using such propaganda to try to "Illuminize" the Islamic world as it did the Western world – marginalizing religion via cultural engineering. However, many Muslims are well aware of the Illuminati's agenda and methodology; they can see from the culture of the modern West where it wants to take their societies, and they have become more sophisticated in resisting it. As poweful as the New World Order's propaganda machine is, Islamists have found ways to break its halo by using its own media against them. For example, there are thousands of youtube videos, twitter accounts, facebook pages and web forums dedicated to spreading Islamist messages and building Islamist communities. Islamists rely on these media to create an alternative propaganda system and propagate opposing narratives. When thousands of people openly express their support for radical jihadist actions and messages on social media, it provides a powerful "social proof" that they are on the winning team. However, since these media are largely built and controlled by Illuminati-aligned elements, the Islamists are at a serious strategic disadvantage. Whether they can overcome this disadvantage with religious fervor, community cohesion and jihadist ruthlessness and ingenuity is unclear, but they have found some innovative ways to resist the NWO propaganda machine that suggest there is a long struggle ahead.

CONCLUSIONS

In this book, we have shown how the world today is being divided into two warring camps: the camp of the Illuminati and the camp of the Islamic State. We have described the origins, worldviews, goals, thought leaders and methodologies of both camps, and the ways they are fighting each other on battlefields across the globe to impose their new world orders. The choice is yours whether to accept this analysis, and whether to choose a side. After the 9/11 attacks, George W. Bush famously declared to the world: "you are either with us, or your with the terrorists". But are these the only choices? Might it be a false choice, or even a vast deception?

A False Dialectic?

There are those who argue that this ISIS vs. Illuminati "war" is totally bogus, and is being manufactured by some diabolical elements within the West – the CIA, Zionist cabals, international bankers, etc. – who are themselves controlled by the Illuminati. Could it be that the ISIS phenomenon, and al-Qaeda before them – which undeniably received Western support in the past – are Illuminati operations designed to advanced its occult agenda of establishing the New World Order? Is the Illuminati using the jihadists as part of an "ordo ab chao" strategy to spread chaos in the Muslim world in order to break down their resistance, or to promote a counterfeit, "Satanic" version of Islam that will discredit the religion in the eyes of the world? Are they employing jihadists as a mercenary force against enemy regimes, such as Assad's Syria, Qadaffi's Libya and Putin's Russia? Do the jihadists serve a useful function by creating a terrorism/counter-terrorism escalating dialectic of fear, allowing the Illuminati's operatives to push through intrusive, totalitarian measures in formerly "free" societies, thus accelerating their program of a totalitarian One World Government? Has a "false dialectic" been created – a situation where a menace has been manufactured and a "problem-reaction-solution" dynamic has been enacted, allowing the masterminds behind the scenes to control the narrative?

There is some evidence for all of these claims, in fact. But after considerable research, it is this author's opinion that a grand Islamist-Illuminati conspiracy is unlikely. There may be elements of the Illuminati (e.g. neocons and Zionists) who consider ISIS a useful buffer against Syria and Iran and aren't aggressively targeting them, but there is no smoking gun showing that ISIS is being actively supported by such elements. The radically anti-Illuminist nature and explosive potential of ISIS makes it difficult to believe that any Illuminati faction would play with that much fire. Nevertheless, I consider this a possibility that can't be ruled out and requires further investigation.

A Cosmic War?

There is a rather grand metaphysical way to look at this conflict between ISIS and the Illuminati that may sound far-fetched, but is fascinating to consider. What if these two organizations really are puppets of opposing cosmic powers? Could it be that ISIS is actually serving the will of a being called Allah – whom the Jews called *Yahweh*, the ancient god of the Israelites? And could this Yahweh really be a rather harsh and tyrannical god, who commands his followers to submit to his laws, punish infidels, wage war and conquer in his name? And on the other side, is there really a being called Lucifer, mortal enemy of Yahweh, who has been trying to "liberate" mankind from Yahweh's rule for thousands of years? And is the Illuminati, who have openly proclaimed their allegiance to Lucifer, serving that being's will, either wittingly or unwittingly? Could there really be a "war in heaven" for control of this world, with human pawns caught in a cosmic game they can scarcely comprehend?

As crazy or sacrilegious as that may sound to some, it does fit the facts in many ways, and give us a theory to work with. For it does seem to this author as if vast cosmic forces are coming to a head in our time, and some great climax or revealing is at hand. At the very least, it gives us an interesting symbolic model for the conflict. All we can do now is watch and wait and learn, and play our fated role in the great drama that is now unfolding.

Final Thoughts

In this book, we have described the ideologies, agendas, strategies and histories of two great global projects which are coming into dramatic conflict in our time. It is a conflict that effects us all, even though we may want no part in it. To paraphrase Leon Trotsky: you may not be interested in the ISIS-Illuminati war, but the ISIS-Illuminati war is interested in you.

For those who aren't in either camp, what is the takeaway here? That is for you to decide, but I'll leave you with this: throughout history, empires, religions and ideas have clashed, drawing millions into their bloody killing fields. Though some will try, none can fully escape these earthly wars, which are manifestations of metaphysical, unearthly power struggles. It is much better, I think, not to attempt an impossible escape, but to build something else that is more to your liking. For the Illuminati-ISIS war may not turn out to be a battle to bring a new dawn to this world, but the twilight struggle of two ideologies whose best days are behind them. Perhaps it is best if these two projects destroy each other, allowing those of us who can imagine other orders, not ruled over by either world-dominating ideology, to quietly begin building the foundations of the next age. Good luck.

APPENDIX A: QUOTES

Below are some quotes from both the Islamists and the Illuminati that substantiate some of the claims made in this book.

Islamist Quotes

"Islam is a revolutionary faith that comes to destroy any government made by man. Islam doesn't look for a nation to be in better condition than another nation. Islam doesn't care about the land or who own the land. The goal of Islam is to rule the entire world and submit all of mankind to the faith of Islam. Any nation or power in this world that tries to get in the way of that goal, Islam will fight and destroy." –*Abul A'la Maududi*

"It is the nature of Islam to dominate, not to be dominated, to impose its law on all nations and to extend its power to the entire planet."

"Islam requires that the Muslim community unite around one leader or one head, the head of the Islamic State, and it forbids the Muslim community from being divided among states."

–*Hassan al-Banna*

"When Islam makes it declaration for the liberation of mankind on earth, so that they may only serve God alone, those who usurp God's authority try to silence it. They will never tolerate it or leave it in peace. Islam will not sit idle either. It will move to deprive them of their power so that people can be freed of their shackles. This is the permanent state of affairs which necessitates the continuity of jihad until all submission is made to God alone."

"It may happen that the enemies of Islam may consider it expedient not to take any action against Islam, if Islam leaves them alone in their geographical boundaries to continue the lordship of some men over others and does not extend its message and its declaration of universal freedom within their domain. But Islam cannot agree to this unless they submit to its authority by paying Jizyah, which will be a guarantee that they have opened their doors for the preaching of Islam and will not put any obstacle in its way through the power of the state."

–Sayyid Qutb

"Al-Qa'idah was set up to wage a jihad against infidelity, particularly to encounter the onslaught of the infidel countries against the Islamic states. Jihad is the sixth undeclared element of Islam. The first five being the basic holy words of Islam, prayers, fast, pilgrimage to Mecca, and giving alms Every anti-Islamic person is afraid of it. Al-Qa'idah wants to keep this element alive and active and make it part of the daily life of the Muslims. It wants to give it the status of worship. We are not against any Islamic country nor do we consider a war against an Islamic country as jihad." –Osama *bin Laden*

"Fighting the devil doesn't require consultation or prayers seeking divine guidance. They are the party of the devils... Fighting them is what is called for at this time. We have reached a point where it is either us or them... We are two opposites that will never come together. What they want can only be accomplished by our elimination. Therefore this is a defining battle." –*Anwar al-Awlaki*

"O ummah of Islam, indeed the world today has been divided into two camps and two trenches, with no third camp present: The camp of Islam and faith, and the camp of kufr (disbelief) and hypocrisy – the camp of the Muslims and the mujahidin everywhere, and the camp of the jews, the crusaders, their allies, and with them the rest of the nations and religions of kufr, all being led by America and Russia, and being mobilized by the jews." –*Abu Bakr Al-Baghdadi*

Illuminati Quotes

"Now, we can see a new world coming into view. A world in which there is the very real prospect of a New World Order. A world where the United Nations, freed from cold war stalemate, is poised to fulfill the historic vision of its founders." – *George H. W. Bush*

"From the days of Spartacus-Weishaupt to those of Karl Marx, to those of Trotsky, Bela Kun, Rosa Luxembourg, and Emma Goldman, this world-wide conspiracy for the overthrow of civilization and for the reconstitution of society on the basis of arrested development, of envious malevolence and impossible equality, has been steadily growing.

It played a definitely recognizable role in the tragedy of the French Revolution. It has been the mainspring of every subversive movement during the nineteenth century, and now at last this band of extraordinary personalities from the underworld of the great cities of Europe and America have gripped the Russian people by the hair of their heads, and have become practically the undisputed masters of that enormous empire." –*Winston Churchill*

"For more than a century, ideological extremists at either end of the political spectrum have seized upon well-publicized incidents to attack the Rockefeller family for the inordinate influence they claim we wield over American political and economic institutions. Some even believe we are part of a secret cabal working against the best interests of the United States, characterizing my family and me as 'internationalists' and of conspiring with others around the world to build a more integrated global political and economic structure – one world, if you will. If that is the charge, I stand guilty, and I am proud of it." –*David Rockefeller*

"We are grateful to the Washington Post, the New York Times, Time magazine, and other great publications whose directors have attended our meetings and respected their promises of discretion for almost forty years. It would have been impossible for us to develop our plan for the world if we had been subject to the bright lights of publicity during these years. But the world is now more sophisticated and prepared to march towards a world government which will never again know war, but only peace and prosperity for the whole of humanity. The supranational sovereignty of an intellectual elite and world bankers is surely preferable to the national auto determination practiced in the past centuries." –*David Rockefeller*

"Since I entered politics, I have chiefly had men's views confided to me privately. Some of the biggest men in the United States, in the field of commerce and manufacture, are afraid of somebody, are afraid of something. They know that there is a power somewhere so organized, so subtle, so watchful, so interlocked, so complete, so pervasive, that they had better not speak above their breath when they speak in condemnation of it." –*Woodrow Wilson*

"By the end of this decade we will live under the first One World Government that has ever existed in the society of nations ... a government with absolute authority to decide the basic issues of human survival. One world government is inevitable." –*Pope John Paul II*

"The Technocratic Age is slowly designing an every day more controlled society. The society will be dominated by an elite of persons free from traditional values who will have no doubt in fulfilling their objectives by means of purged techniques with which they will influence the behavior of people and will control and watch the society in all details. ... it will become possible to exert a practically permanent watch on each citizen of the world."

"This regionalization is in keeping with the Tri-Lateral Plan which calls for a gradual convergence of East and West, ultimately leading toward the goal of one world government. National sovereignty is no longer a viable concept."

–Zbigniew Brzezinski, co-founder of the Trilateral Commission

"The powers of financial capitalism had another far-reaching aim, nothing less than to create a world system of financial control in private hands able to dominate the political system of each country and the economy of the world as a whole. This system was to be controlled in a feudalist fashion by the central banks of the world acting in concert, by secret agreements arrived at in frequent private meetings and conferences." *–Carroll Quigley*

"We will have a world government whether you like it or not. The only question is whether that government will be achieved by conquest or consent." *–Paul Warburg*

"With the exception of the U.S.S.R. as a federated Eurasian State, all other continents will become united in a world alliance at whose disposal will be an international police force. All armies will be abolished and there will be no more wars. In Jerusalem, the United Nations will build a shrine of the prophets to serve the federated union of all continents; this will be the seat of the Supreme Court of Mankind, to settle all controversies among the federated continents, as prophesied by Isaiah..." *–David Ben-Gurion*

APPENDIX B: RESOLUTION ON FREEMASONRY

The First Fiqh Council Resolution on Freemasonry

The following resolution was made in 1978, when the Muslim World League's Fiqh Council released "The First Resolution on Freemasonry and Affiliation with It", in which they condemned the Freemasons as a suversive, un-Islamic, pro-Zionist organization. The Resolution is important enough for the topic of this book that we reproduce it below.

The Islamic Fiqh Council during its 1st session held in Makkah Mukarramah, Saudi Arabia between 10-17 Sha'ban 1398H discussed the Freemasonry and those who associate with it. It also discussed the ruling of Islamic Shari'ah concerning it.

The members of the Council made a detailed study about this dangerous organization and its literature written by its own members and leading personalities as well as other old and new publications about it, and arrived at the following conclusions:

1. Freemasonry is a secret organization, concealing or revealing itself, according to the circumstances of time and place. However, its real principles are based on secrecy in all circumstances. They are not known even to its members except those who have reached its higher ranks after passing through various experiences.

2. It builds the relationship of its members in all parts of the world on superficial basis in order to dupe the simple-minded people. It pretends to establish a human fraternity among those who join it, without differentiation between various ideologies, creeds or religions.

3. It attracts the important people to its organization and lures them through the temptation of personal benefits, on the basis that each member of the organization is supposed to help the other member anywhere in the world with his needs and problems and supports him to achieve his aims if he has any political ambition. This is the greatest temptation through which, they attract the influential people in the society. It also receives financial contributions from them.

4. Affiliation to this organization is based on ceremonial entry of the new member under certain norms by which a new member is threatened in case he violates the instructions or orders issued to him through the senior ranks.

5. The simple-minded members are left free to practise their own religious rites, while the organization benefits from them to the extent of their utility, keeping them in lower ranks. On the other hand, apostates or those show readiness for apostasy are promoted gradually to the higher ranks in

the light of the member's experiences and frequent tests that show their ability to serve its dangerous plans and principles.

6. It has certain political aims and has been involved overtly or covertly in some major military coups and political changes in the world.

7. In its origin and essence, this organization has Jewish roots and it is controlled secretly by a higher worldwide Jewish management. In its activities, it has a Zionist outlook.

8. In its real aims, it is against all religions. It undermines them in general and aims at tarnishing the religion of Islam in particular in the eyes of its followers.

9. It is always keen to select its members from the people who enjoy the outstanding academic, social, political, financial or any other status, so that it can effectively exploit their influence in their respective societies. That is why it is so keen to attract persons such as kings, presidents, ministers and senior government officials.

10. It has many branches that take different names in order to deceive and direct the people's attention away from it. This way, it can carry out its activities under different names if it is met with resistance to the name of Freemasonry in certain environment. The branches which work under different names are most prominently known as Lions, Rotary and other outfits which harbour the sinister aims and activities that are totally against the foundations of Islam.

It has become very clear to the Islamic Fiqh Council

that there is a strong relationship between Freemasonry and International Zionist Movement. That is why it was able to control the activities of many officials in the Arab and non-Arab countries, especially with regard to the issue of Palestine, obstructing their crucial roles for this great cause in the favour of Jews and International Zionist Movement.

For this and other detailed information about the sinister aims and activities of Freemasonry, the Islamic Fiqh Council decides that Freemasonry is one of the most dangerous organizations which aim at the destruction of Islam and Muslims, and that whoever associates with it, knowing its reality and objectives is an unbeliever.

ABOUT THE AUTHORS

The Dark Lords are the masters of their own occult Order that is not aligned with any Illuminati faction nor with the Islamists. They have founded various schools and cults to propagate their ideas and educate new generations of students of power. The Dark Lords have a passion for getting to the root of the religions, ideologies, metaphysical forces and power structures that rule our world. They are in the process of publishing a series of books for aspiring Dark Lords on a wide variety of subjects: religion, politics, occultism, philosophy, psychology, mind power, covert operations, martial arts, military strategy and more. These books form the core curriculum of their schools, and lay the intellectual foundations of the new Empire they are bringing to this world.

For more information about the Dark Lords' many books and projects, visit **thedarklords.com**.